YouTube Marketing

The Ultimate Guide to Viral Video Strategies for Building Your Brand, Growing Your Audience, Increasing Engagement, and Boosting Sales with Video Content

Heinrich Brevis

Table of Contents

Introduction

In today's digital age, video content reigns supreme. As the world's second-largest search engine and the most popular video-sharing platform, YouTube has transformed how we consume information, entertain ourselves, and make purchasing decisions. With over 2 billion logged-in monthly users, the potential reach of a successful YouTube marketing strategy is unparalleled. Whether you're a budding entrepreneur, an established business owner, or a content creator looking to amplify your influence, YouTube offers a dynamic and engaging way to connect with your audience, build your brand, and drive sales.

Welcome to "YouTube Marketing: The Ultimate Guide to Viral Video Strategies for Building Your Brand, Growing Your Audience, Increasing Engagement, and Boosting Sales with Video Content." This book is your comprehensive resource for navigating the complex yet rewarding world of YouTube marketing. Here, you'll find everything you need to turn your video ideas into successful marketing campaigns that captivate viewers and convert them into loyal customers.

The Power of YouTube

The statistics speak for themselves: YouTube is a juggernaut in the online world. With millions of hours of content uploaded every minute, the platform has something for everyone, from how-to tutorials and product reviews to vlogs and web series. But beyond just content consumption, YouTube is a powerful tool for businesses and creators to build a personal connection with their audience, foster community, and establish authority in their niche.

Why YouTube Marketing?

You might wonder, why focus on YouTube marketing when so many other platforms are available? The answer lies in the unique advantages that YouTube offers:

- **Visual Storytelling**: Video allows you to convey your brand's story more engagingly and memorably than text or static images.
- **SEO Benefits**: Owned by Google, YouTube videos often rank high in search results, significantly boosting your visibility and discoverability.
- **Monetization Opportunities**: Beyond ad revenue, YouTube offers numerous ways to monetize your content, from sponsored videos and product placements to membership programs and merchandise.
- **Community Building**: The interactive nature of YouTube fosters a sense of community, enabling direct communication with your audience through comments, likes, and shares.
- **Analytics and Insights**: YouTube's robust analytics tools help you understand your audience's behavior, preferences, and engagement patterns, allowing for continuous improvement of your content strategy.

What You'll Learn

This book is designed to be your ultimate guide to mastering YouTube marketing, regardless of your current level of expertise. Here's a sneak peek of what you'll discover:

- **Creating Compelling Content**: Learn the art of storytelling and content creation that captivates viewers and keeps them coming back for more.
- **Optimizing for SEO**: Unlock the secrets of YouTube's search algorithm and discover how to optimize your videos for maximum reach and visibility.
- **Building Your Brand**: Understand the importance of brand consistency and how to develop a recognizable and trustworthy brand presence on YouTube.
- **Growing Your Audience**: Discover proven strategies for attracting and retaining subscribers, from leveraging social media to collaborating with other creators.
- **Increasing Engagement**: Explore techniques to boost viewer interaction, including calls to action, community posts, and live streaming.
- **Driving Sales**: Learn how to create videos that not only entertain but also convert, driving traffic to your website and increasing sales.

The Journey Ahead

Embarking on your YouTube marketing journey can feel daunting, but with the right guidance and strategies, it can also be incredibly rewarding. This book is here to provide you with the insights, tips, and tools you need to succeed. Whether you're looking to launch your first video or take your existing channel to new heights, "YouTube Marketing: The Ultimate Guide to Viral Video Strategies for Building Your Brand, Growing Your Audience, Increasing Engagement, and Boosting Sales with Video Content" will be your trusted companion every step of the way.

So, are you ready to harness the power of YouTube and transform your brand's digital presence? Let's dive in and start creating videos that not only go viral but also drive real business results. Welcome to the world of YouTube marketing!

Chapter 1: Introduction to YouTube Marketing

In a world where digital consumption is at an all-time high, video content has emerged as the king of the internet. From tutorials and reviews to vlogs and documentaries, videos captivate and engage audiences like no other medium. At the forefront of this video revolution stands YouTube, a platform that has redefined how we share and consume content. For businesses and content creators alike, YouTube is not just a platform—it's a powerful tool for marketing, brand building, and audience engagement.

Understanding YouTube's Impact

Since its inception in 2005, YouTube has grown exponentially. What started as a platform for sharing personal videos has transformed into a global phenomenon, boasting over 2 billion logged-in monthly users and billions of views every single day. This staggering reach makes YouTube an indispensable channel for marketers looking to tap into a diverse and engaged audience.

YouTube's impact goes beyond mere numbers. It has changed the way people discover and interact with brands. Users turn to YouTube for information, entertainment, and inspiration. They watch product reviews before making purchasing decisions, follow tutorials to learn new skills and subscribe to channels that resonate with their interests and values. For marketers, this means an unparalleled opportunity to reach potential customers in a highly engaging and personal way.

Why Choose YouTube for Marketing?

The question isn't whether you should use YouTube for marketing, but why you shouldn't. Here are some compelling reasons why YouTube should be at the heart of your digital marketing strategy:

- **Massive Reach**: With billions of users across the globe, YouTube provides access to a vast and diverse audience. Whether you're targeting teenagers, young adults, or professionals, you can find your audience on YouTube.
- **Engaging Format**: Video content is inherently engaging. It combines visual and auditory elements to tell compelling stories, demonstrate products, and convey messages more effectively than text or images alone.
- **Search Engine Optimization (SEO)**: YouTube is the second-largest search engine in the world, right after Google. By optimizing your videos for SEO, you can increase your chances of appearing in search results, driving organic traffic to your content.
- **Monetization Options**: YouTube offers various monetization options, from ad revenue and channel memberships to Super Chats and merchandise shelves. These features allow creators to generate income while building their brand.
- **Analytics and Insights**: YouTube provides detailed analytics that help you understand your audience's behavior and preferences. These insights enable you to refine your content strategy and create videos that resonate with your viewers.
- **Community Building**: YouTube fosters a sense of community through features like comments, likes, and shares. Engaging with your audience in these ways helps build a loyal and interactive community around your brand.

The Core Elements of YouTube Marketing

To succeed on YouTube, you need a well-rounded strategy that encompasses various elements of video creation and marketing. Here are the core components you'll explore in this book:

- **Content Creation**: The foundation of any successful YouTube channel is high-quality content. You'll learn how to create videos that are visually appealing, informative, and aligned with your brand's message.
- **SEO Optimization**: Discover the techniques for optimizing your videos to rank higher in YouTube search results. This includes keyword research, compelling titles, descriptions, tags, and thumbnails.
- **Audience Engagement**: Building a strong relationship with your audience is crucial. You'll find strategies for encouraging viewer interaction, responding to comments, and fostering a sense of community
- **Brand Building**: Consistency is key to brand recognition. Learn how to maintain a cohesive brand identity across your channel, from visual elements to your tone of voice.
- **Promotion and Distribution**: Creating great content is just the beginning. You'll also need to promote your videos through social media, collaborations, and other marketing channels to reach a wider audience.
- **Monetization**: Once you've built a solid following, explore the various monetization options available on YouTube to turn your channel into a revenue-generating asset.

Setting Goals and Defining Success

Before diving into the nitty-gritty of YouTube marketing, it's important to define what success looks like for you. Are you aiming to build brand awareness, generate leads, drive sales, or simply grow your subscriber base? Setting clear, measurable goals will help you stay focused and track your progress.

Consider using the SMART criteria to set your goals: Specific, Measurable, Achievable, Relevant, and Time-bound. For example, instead of setting a vague goal like "increase subscribers," aim to "gain 1,000 new subscribers within three months by posting two high-quality videos per week and engaging with viewers in the comments."

The Journey Ahead

As you embark on your YouTube marketing journey, remember that success doesn't happen overnight. It requires dedication, creativity, and a willingness to learn and adapt. This book will provide you with the knowledge and tools you need to navigate the complexities of YouTube marketing and achieve your goals.

In the chapters that follow, you'll delve deeper into each aspect of YouTube marketing, from creating compelling content and optimizing for SEO to building your brand and monetizing your channel. Whether you're a beginner or an experienced marketer, this comprehensive guide will equip you with the strategies and insights to make the most of YouTube's powerful platform.

1.1 The Power of YouTube in the Digital Age

In the digital age, few platforms have reshaped the landscape of media and marketing as profoundly as YouTube. From its humble beginnings in 2005 to becoming a cornerstone of online culture and commerce, YouTube has revolutionized the way we consume content, interact with brands, and make purchasing decisions. Understanding the power of YouTube is essential for anyone looking to harness its potential for marketing success.

A Global Audience at Your Fingertips

One of YouTube's most significant advantages is its massive global reach. With over 2 billion logged-in monthly users, the platform spans every demographic imaginable. This vast user base includes people of all ages, backgrounds, and interests, providing marketers with an unparalleled opportunity to connect with a diverse audience.

Unlike traditional media, YouTube allows for precise targeting. Advanced algorithms and analytics enable you to reach specific segments of the population based on their viewing habits, search history, and engagement patterns. Whether you're targeting teenagers interested in the latest fashion trends or professionals seeking industry insights, YouTube offers the tools to reach your ideal audience effectively.

Engaging and Memorable Content

Video content's dynamic nature makes it uniquely engaging. It combines visuals, sound, and storytelling to create a multi-sensory experience that captures attention and leaves a lasting impression. This is particularly important in a world where consumers are bombarded with information from multiple sources.

YouTube's format allows for a variety of content types that can cater to different marketing objectives. Product demonstrations, tutorials, behind-the-scenes looks, customer testimonials, and live streams are just a few examples of how brands can use video to engage their audience. The ability to create content that resonates emotionally and visually enhances your brand's message and encourages viewers to take action.

Enhanced Visibility through SEO

YouTube is the second-largest search engine globally, second only to Google, which owns it. This relationship means that YouTube videos often rank highly in Google search results, providing a significant SEO advantage. By optimizing your video content with relevant keywords, compelling titles, descriptions, and tags, you can improve your chances of appearing in both YouTube and Google search results.

This enhanced visibility is crucial for driving organic traffic to your content. Users searching for information or solutions related to your industry can discover your videos, leading to increased brand awareness and new customer acquisition. Effective SEO practices can turn YouTube into a powerful tool for attracting and converting potential customers.

Monetization and Revenue Opportunities

Beyond brand building and audience engagement, YouTube offers numerous monetization opportunities. For content creators and businesses alike, these options provide ways to generate revenue directly from the platform. Here are some of the primary monetization methods available on YouTube:

- **Ad Revenue**: Through the YouTube Partner Program, creators can earn money from ads displayed on their videos. The more views and engagement your videos receive, the higher your potential ad revenue.
- **Channel Memberships**: This feature allows creators to offer exclusive perks and content to subscribers who pay a monthly fee. It's an excellent way to generate recurring income while providing additional value to your most dedicated fans.
- **Super Chat and Super Stickers**: During live streams, viewers can purchase Super Chats and Super Stickers to highlight their messages. This not only enhances viewer engagement but also provides a direct revenue stream for creators.
- **Merchandise Shelf**: YouTube enables creators to showcase and sell merchandise directly from their channel. This integration makes it easy for fans to purchase branded products without leaving the platform.
- **Sponsorships and Brand Deals**: Collaborating with brands for sponsored content is another lucrative avenue. Companies are willing to pay creators to promote their products or services, especially if the creator's audience aligns with their target market.

Building a Community

One of YouTube's most powerful aspects is its ability to foster a sense of community. Unlike other platforms where interaction is often limited to likes and shares, YouTube encourages deeper engagement through comments, community posts, and live interactions. This sense of community can be a game-changer for your brand.

Engaging with your audience by responding to comments, hosting Q&A sessions, and acknowledging viewer contributions helps build a loyal and interactive community. This not only strengthens your relationship with your audience but also increases the likelihood of viewers becoming brand advocates who promote your content organically.

Real-Time Analytics and Insights

Understanding your audience and their behavior is crucial for refining your marketing strategy. YouTube provides robust analytics tools that offer insights into various metrics, such as watch time, audience demographics, traffic sources, and engagement rates. These analytics allow you to track the performance of your videos and identify trends that can inform your content strategy.

By analyzing these metrics, you can gain a deeper understanding of what resonates with your audience, which types of content perform best, and how viewers are finding and interacting with your videos. This data-driven approach enables continuous improvement and helps you make informed decisions to optimize your YouTube marketing efforts.

The Future of YouTube Marketing

As technology continues to evolve, so too will the opportunities and challenges of YouTube marketing. The platform is constantly innovating, introducing new features and tools that can enhance your marketing strategy. Staying updated with these changes and adapting to new trends will be crucial for maintaining a competitive edge.

1.2 Why Video Marketing Matters

In the fast-paced, content-saturated world of digital marketing, capturing and retaining the attention of your audience is more challenging than ever. Text and images alone often struggle to make a lasting impact. Enter video marketing—a powerful medium that has transformed the way brands communicate with their audiences. Understanding why video marketing matters is crucial for anyone looking to enhance their digital strategy and achieve meaningful engagement and conversion.

The Rise of Video Consumption

Video content has exploded in popularity over the past decade. With the advent of faster internet speeds, mobile technology, and platforms like YouTube, consumers now expect high-quality video content as a part of their online experience. The statistics are compelling:

- **High Engagement Rates**: Videos attract more engagement than any other type of content. They are more likely to be liked, shared, and commented on compared to text-based posts or static images.
- **Increased Consumption**: According to recent studies, the average person watches over 100 minutes of online video every day. This trend shows no signs of slowing down as more people turn to video for information and entertainment.

- **Preferred Content-Type**: Consumers prefer video content for its ease of consumption and the immersive experience it provides. Whether it's product reviews, tutorials, or entertainment, video meets the audience's needs in a way that text cannot.

The Psychological Impact of Video

Video's effectiveness can be partly attributed to its ability to engage multiple senses simultaneously. This multi-sensory experience enhances message retention and emotional connection. Here's why video has such a strong psychological impact:

- **Visual and Auditory Stimulation**: Videos engage both visual and auditory senses, making it easier for viewers to remember information. The combination of moving images and sound helps in creating a more memorable experience.
- **Emotional Connection**: Video storytelling can evoke emotions more effectively than written content. Music, voice tone, facial expressions, and visuals work together to convey emotions, making the content more relatable and impactful.
- **Narrative and Storytelling**: Humans are hardwired to respond to stories. Video allows brands to tell their stories compellingly, creating a narrative that resonates with viewers and fosters a deeper connection.

Benefits of Video Marketing

Incorporating video into your marketing strategy offers numerous benefits that can significantly enhance your brand's online presence and effectiveness:

- **Improved SEO**: Search engines prioritize video content. Having videos on your website can improve your search engine rankings, increase visibility, and drive more traffic. YouTube, being the second-largest search engine, provides an added advantage for SEO when your videos are optimized correctly.
- **Higher Conversion Rates**: Video content is highly effective at converting viewers into customers. Studies have shown that landing pages with videos can increase conversion rates by up to 80%. Product videos, testimonials, and explainer videos can provide the information needed to persuade viewers to make a purchase.
- **Enhanced Brand Awareness**: Videos have a higher shareability factor. Engaging and informative videos are more likely to be shared on social media, extending your brand's reach and increasing awareness. This virality aspect can significantly boost your brand's visibility and reputation.
- **Greater Engagement**: Videos capture attention more effectively than text or images. They can keep viewers engaged for longer periods, reducing bounce rates and increasing time spent on your site or channel. Interactive elements like annotations, end screens, and call-to-action buttons further enhance engagement.
- **Versatility Across Platforms**: Video content is versatile and can be repurposed across various platforms. From YouTube and Facebook to Instagram and TikTok, video can be tailored to suit the specific requirements and audience preferences of each platform, maximizing its reach and impact.

- **Personalization**: Video allows for a high degree of personalization. Personalized video messages, product recommendations, and targeted video ads can significantly enhance customer experience and drive engagement.

The Competitive Edge

In today's competitive digital landscape, businesses that leverage video marketing have a distinct advantage. Video content not only captures attention but also builds trust and credibility. Consumers are more likely to trust a brand that provides clear, informative, and engaging video content. This trust translates into customer loyalty and repeat business.

Additionally, video marketing allows brands to stand out in a crowded market. High-quality videos reflect a level of professionalism and commitment to providing value to your audience. They showcase your brand's personality, values, and unique selling points more effectively than other content formats.

Integrating Video into Your Marketing Strategy

To fully capitalize on the power of video marketing, it's essential to integrate it seamlessly into your overall marketing strategy. Here are some steps to get started:

- **Define Your Goals**: Determine what you want to achieve with your video marketing efforts. Whether it's increasing brand awareness, driving sales, or improving customer engagement, having clear goals will guide your strategy.

- **Understand Your Audience**: Know your audience's preferences, pain points, and behaviors. This understanding will help you create content that resonates and meets their needs.
- **Create High-Quality Content**: Invest in quality production to ensure your videos are professional and engaging. This doesn't always mean a high budget—creativity and authenticity are key.
- **Optimize for SEO**: Use relevant keywords, compelling titles, descriptions, and tags to optimize your videos for search engines. This will help improve your visibility and attract organic traffic.
- **Promote Your Videos**: Share your videos across multiple platforms, including social media, your website, and email marketing campaigns. Collaborate with influencers and encourage viewers to share your content.
- **Analyze and Adapt**: Use analytics tools to measure the performance of your videos. Monitor metrics like views, engagement, and conversion rates. Use these insights to refine your strategy and create even more effective content.

The Future of Video Marketing

As technology continues to evolve, so will the possibilities for video marketing. Virtual reality (VR), augmented reality (AR), and interactive video experiences are on the rise, offering new and innovative ways to engage with audiences. Staying ahead of these trends and continually adapting your video marketing strategy will be crucial for long-term success.

1.3 Understanding the YouTube Algorithm

The YouTube algorithm is a sophisticated system that determines which videos are recommended to viewers and how videos rank in search results. For marketers and content creators, understanding how this algorithm works is crucial for optimizing videos and maximizing their reach and engagement. In this section, we will demystify the YouTube algorithm and provide insights into how you can leverage it to your advantage.

The Evolution of the YouTube Algorithm

Over the years, the YouTube algorithm has undergone significant changes to improve user experience and ensure that viewers receive relevant and engaging content. Initially, YouTube focused heavily on view counts. The more views a video had, the more likely it was to be recommended. However, this approach had its flaws, as it led to clickbait and low-quality content.

Today, the algorithm is much more sophisticated, taking into account various signals to determine the quality and relevance of a video. YouTube aims to keep viewers on the platform longer by recommending videos that match their interests and preferences.

Key Components of the YouTube Algorithm

1. Watch Time and Session Time:

- **Watch Time** refers to the total amount of time viewers spend watching your videos. Longer watch times indicate that your content is engaging and valuable.
- **Session Time** extends beyond individual videos, referring to the amount of time a user spends on YouTube during a single visit. If your videos contribute to longer session times by keeping viewers engaged on the platform, the algorithm rewards you with better visibility.

2. Click-Through Rate (CTR):

CTR measures how often viewers click on your video after seeing the thumbnail and title. A higher CTR suggests that your video is appealing and relevant to the audience. Thumbnails and titles should be compelling and accurately represent the content to boost CTR.

3. Engagement Metrics:

The algorithm considers likes, comments, shares, and subscriptions as indicators of viewer engagement. High engagement signals that your content resonates with viewers, which can improve its ranking.

4. Video Retention:

Video retention refers to how much of your video viewers watch. High retention rates indicate that your content is holding viewers' attention.

The algorithm favors videos that keep viewers engaged from start to finish.

5. User Personalization:

The algorithm tailors recommendations based on individual user behavior. It takes into account past watch history, search queries, and interaction patterns to deliver personalized content. Ensuring your content is relevant to your target audience enhances its likelihood of being recommended.

6. Video Metadata:

Titles, descriptions, tags, and closed captions are essential for SEO. Including relevant keywords helps the algorithm understand your content and match it with user queries. Detailed and accurate metadata improves your video's discoverability.

Strategies to Optimize for the YouTube Algorithm

To succeed on YouTube, it's important to create content that not only appeals to viewers but also aligns with the algorithm's preferences. Here are some strategies to optimize your videos:

1. Create High-Quality, Engaging Content:

Focus on producing content that provides value to your audience. This could be educational, entertaining, or inspirational content that keeps viewers engaged and coming back for more.

2. Optimize Video Metadata:

Conduct keyword research to identify relevant terms and phrases your target audience is searching for. Include these keywords naturally in your video title, description, and tags. Craft compelling titles and descriptions that encourage clicks while accurately representing the content.

3. Design Attractive Thumbnails:

Thumbnails are the first thing viewers see, so make them eye-catching and relevant. Use high-quality images, bold text, and contrasting colors to stand out. A good thumbnail can significantly boost your CTR and attract more viewers to your videos.

4. Encourage Viewer Interaction:

Prompt viewers to like, comment, and share your videos. Ask questions, solicit feedback, and engage with viewers in the comments section. Higher interaction rates signal to the algorithm that your content is valuable and engaging.

5. Increase Watch Time and Retention:

Structure your videos to retain viewers' attention. Start with a strong hook to capture interest within the first few seconds. Maintain a clear and engaging narrative throughout, and avoid unnecessary fluff that might cause viewers to drop off.

6. Publish Consistently:

Regular uploads can help you maintain and grow your audience. Establish a consistent posting schedule so viewers know when to expect new content from you. Consistency helps build viewer loyalty and increases the chances of your videos being recommended.

7. Promote Your Videos Across Channels:

Share your videos on social media, embed them in blog posts, and include them in email newsletters. The more views and engagement your video receives early on, the more likely it is to be picked up by the algorithm and recommended to a broader audience.

8. Leverage Playlists:

Organize your videos into playlists to encourage binge-watching. Playlists help increase session time by keeping viewers on your channel longer, which is favorable for the algorithm. Group similar content together to create a seamless viewing experience.

9. Utilize End Screens and Cards:

End screens and cards are effective tools to promote additional content within your videos. Use them to direct viewers to other videos, playlists, or your subscription button, thereby increasing overall watch time and engagement.

10. Analyze Performance and Adapt:

Regularly review your analytics to understand which videos are performing well and why. Pay attention to metrics like watch time, retention, CTR, and engagement. Use these insights to refine your content strategy and create videos that better meet your audience's needs and preferences.

The Role of External Factors

While the YouTube algorithm primarily focuses on on-platform behavior, external factors can also influence your video's performance. Promoting your videos through other channels, such as social media, blogs, and email marketing, can drive initial traffic and engagement, which can positively impact how the algorithm views your content.

Collaborations with other YouTubers or influencers can also be beneficial. Partnering with creators who have a similar or complementary audience can introduce your content to new viewers, increase your subscriber base, and enhance your video's performance metrics.

Staying Updated with Algorithm Changes

The YouTube algorithm is continually evolving, and staying updated with its changes is essential for long-term success. YouTube frequently updates its algorithm to improve user experience and combat issues like clickbait, misinformation, and low-quality content. Keeping an eye on updates from YouTube, industry news, and insights from successful creators can help you adapt your strategy accordingly.

Understanding the YouTube algorithm is a critical aspect of developing a successful video marketing strategy. By creating high-quality, engaging content and optimizing it according to the algorithm's preferences, you can significantly increase your visibility, reach, and engagement on the platform. Remember, the ultimate goal of the algorithm is to keep viewers satisfied and engaged, so always prioritize providing value to your audience. As you continue to learn and adapt, you'll be well-equipped to harness the power of the YouTube algorithm to achieve your marketing objectives.

1.4 Setting Your Goals: Brand Awareness, Audience Growth, Engagement, and Sales

Setting clear, measurable goals is the cornerstone of any successful YouTube marketing strategy. Goals provide direction, focus, and a benchmark for evaluating success. Whether you are a business looking to enhance brand visibility, a creator aiming to grow your audience, or an entrepreneur wanting to boost sales, establishing well-defined goals will help you stay on track and achieve your objectives. In this section, we'll explore four primary goals you can set for your YouTube channel: brand awareness, audience growth, engagement, and sales.

Brand Awareness

Brand awareness is about ensuring that your target audience recognizes and remembers your brand. On YouTube, this means creating content that effectively communicates your brand's values, personality, and offerings.

1. Define Your Brand Identity:

Understand and articulate what your brand stands for. What are your core values, mission, and unique selling propositions? Consistently convey these elements in your video content.

2. Consistent Branding:

Use consistent visual and auditory branding elements such as logos, color schemes, and music. This helps reinforce your brand identity and makes your videos instantly recognizable.

3. Tell Your Story:

Use videos to share your brand's story. This could include behind-the-scenes looks, founder stories, and insights into your brand's journey. Authentic storytelling fosters a deeper connection with your audience.

4. Increase Visibility:

Utilize SEO strategies to ensure your videos appear in search results. Collaborate with influencers and other brands to reach a wider audience. Paid advertising on YouTube can also boost your brand's visibility to new viewers.

Audience Growth

Growing your audience is crucial for long-term success on YouTube. A larger audience means more views, higher engagement, and greater influence.

1. Know Your Audience:

Conduct market research to understand your target audience's demographics, interests, and viewing habits. Create content that caters to their preferences and solves their problems.

2. Regular and Consistent Posting:

Develop a content calendar and stick to a regular posting schedule. Consistency helps retain your current audience and attract new subscribers.

3. Optimize for Discovery:

Use keywords, tags, and compelling thumbnails to make your videos easily discoverable. Create eye-catching titles and detailed descriptions to attract clicks.

4. Collaborations and Cross-Promotions:

Partner with other YouTubers or brands to tap into their audience base. Cross-promotions can introduce your content to new viewers and encourage them to subscribe.

5. Engage with Your Community:

Respond to comments, ask for feedback, and create interactive content. Engaging with your viewers makes them feel valued and more likely to stick around.

Engagement

Engagement metrics such as likes, comments, shares, and watch time are crucial indicators of how well your content resonates with viewers. High engagement boosts your video's visibility and encourages deeper connections with your audience.

1. Create Interactive Content:

Use polls, Q&A sessions, and live streams to engage your audience directly. Interactive content encourages viewers to participate and share their opinions.

2. Encourage Comments and Shares:

Prompt viewers to like, comment, and share your videos. Asking questions or encouraging discussions at the end of your videos can increase comment rates.

3. Monitor and Respond to Feedback:

Pay attention to the feedback you receive in comments and messages. Respond promptly and thoughtfully to show that you value your audience's input.

4. Build a Community:

Foster a sense of community by creating content that resonates with your audience's interests and values. Use community posts to keep your audience engaged between video uploads.

Sales

Ultimately, many businesses use YouTube to drive sales. Whether you're selling products, services, or digital content, YouTube can be an effective platform for converting viewers into customers.

1. Product Demos and Tutorials:

Create detailed product demonstrations and how-to tutorials. Showcasing your products in action helps potential customers understand their benefits and uses.

2. Customer Testimonials and Reviews:

Share testimonials and reviews from satisfied customers. Social proof can significantly influence purchasing decisions.

3. Clear Calls-to-Action (CTAs):

Include clear and compelling CTAs in your videos. Direct viewers to your website, product pages, or special offers. Use annotations and end screens to make it easy for viewers to take the next step.

4. Promotional Campaigns:

Run exclusive promotions or discounts for your YouTube audience. Limited-time offers can create a sense of urgency and drive sales.

5. Track Conversions:

Use tracking links and YouTube Analytics to monitor the effectiveness of your sales-driven videos. Analyzing conversion data helps refine your strategy and improve future campaigns.

Measuring Success

For each goal, it's essential to define specific, measurable objectives. Use the SMART criteria—Specific, Measurable, Achievable, Relevant, and Time-bound—to set clear targets. For example:

- **Brand Awareness**: Increase the number of unique viewers by 20% over the next six months.
- **Audience Growth**: Gain 1,000 new subscribers within three months.
- **Engagement**: Boost average video watch time by 15% in the next quarter.
- **Sales**: Achieve a 10% increase in sales attributed to YouTube videos over the next fiscal year.

Regularly review your progress using YouTube Analytics and other tracking tools. Adjust your strategies based on what's working and what's not. Flexibility and continuous improvement are key to achieving your YouTube marketing goals.

Setting clear goals is the foundation of a successful YouTube marketing strategy. Whether your focus is on brand awareness, audience growth, engagement, or sales, having well-defined objectives will guide your efforts and help you measure your success. As you proceed with your YouTube journey, keep these goals in mind and use them to shape your content and strategy. By doing so, you'll be well on your way to leveraging the full potential of YouTube to achieve your marketing objectives.

1.5 Essential Tools and Resources for YouTube Marketing

To succeed in YouTube marketing, having the right tools and resources at your disposal is crucial. These tools can help you create high-quality content, optimize your videos for search, analyze performance, and engage with your audience effectively. In this section, we'll explore a range of essential tools and resources that can enhance your YouTube marketing efforts.

Video Creation and Editing Tools

Creating professional, engaging videos is the foundation of a successful YouTube channel. Here are some tools to help you produce high-quality video content:

1. Adobe Premiere Pro:

A leading video editing software used by professionals. It offers advanced features like multi-cam editing, motion graphics, and color correction. It's suitable for both beginners and advanced users.

2. Final Cut Pro:

A powerful video editing tool for Mac users. It provides robust editing capabilities, including 360-degree video editing, HDR support, and advanced color grading.

3. iMovie:

A beginner-friendly video editing software for Mac users. It offers basic editing features, including trimming, transitions, and adding text, making it ideal for new creators.

4. Filmora:

An easy-to-use video editor with a range of effects, filters, and overlays. It's perfect for those who want to create professional-looking videos without a steep learning curve.

5. Camtasia:

A screen recording and video editing tool ideal for creating tutorials, demos, and presentations. It offers a simple interface and useful features like annotations and transitions.

6. Canva:

Primarily known for graphic design, Canva also offers video editing capabilities. It's excellent for creating engaging thumbnails, social media posts, and simple video content.

Audio and Music Resources

High-quality audio is essential for creating professional videos. These tools and resources can help you enhance your video's sound quality:

1. Audacity:

A free, open-source audio editing software. It offers features like noise reduction, equalization, and audio effects, making it ideal for improving sound quality.

2. Adobe Audition:

A professional audio editing software with advanced features like multi-track editing, sound removal, and audio restoration. It's suitable for creating polished, high-quality audio tracks.

3. Epidemic Sound:

A subscription-based service providing access to a vast library of royalty-free music and sound effects. It's perfect for adding professional music to your videos without copyright issues.

4. AudioJungle:

A marketplace for royalty-free music and sound effects. You can purchase individual tracks to enhance your videos with high-quality audio.

Graphic Design Tools

Creating compelling thumbnails, channel art, and graphics is essential for attracting viewers and maintaining a professional appearance:

1. Canva:

A user-friendly design tool that offers templates for YouTube thumbnails, channel art, and social media graphics. It's perfect for non-designers looking to create professional visuals.

2. Adobe Photoshop:

A powerful graphic design software for creating custom thumbnails, channel art, and other visual elements. It's ideal for advanced users who need detailed control over their designs.

3. PicMonkey:

A design tool that offers easy-to-use templates for YouTube graphics. It's great for creating visually appealing thumbnails and social media images quickly.

SEO and Analytics Tools

Optimizing your videos for search and understanding your performance metrics are crucial for growing your channel:

1. TubeBuddy:

A browser extension that offers keyword research, tag suggestions, and SEO optimization tools. It also provides insights into your channel's performance and competitors' strategies.

2. vidIQ:

A YouTube-certified tool that provides keyword research, trend alerts, and detailed analytics. It helps you optimize your videos for better visibility and engagement.

3. Google Analytics:

Integrating Google Analytics with your YouTube channel can provide deeper insights into your audience's behavior, traffic sources, and engagement metrics.

4. YouTube Analytics:

Built into YouTube, this tool provides comprehensive data on your channel's performance, including watch time, audience demographics, traffic sources, and engagement metrics. Use this data to refine your strategy and improve your content.

Collaboration and Promotion Tools

Promoting your videos and collaborating with other creators can help you reach a broader audience:

1. Hootsuite:

A social media management tool that allows you to schedule posts, track performance, and manage multiple social media accounts. It's ideal for promoting your YouTube videos across different platforms.

2. Buffer:

Another social media management tool that helps you schedule posts and analyze engagement. It's useful for maintaining a consistent presence on social media and driving traffic to your YouTube channel.

3. Collab space:

A platform that connects YouTubers for collaboration opportunities. It helps you find other creators to work with, expanding your reach and audience.

4. Gleam:

A promotional tool that helps you run contests and giveaways. It's effective for increasing engagement, gaining subscribers, and promoting your videos.

Educational Resources

Continuously learning and staying updated with the latest trends and strategies in YouTube marketing is essential:

1. YouTube Creator Academy:

An official resource from YouTube offering free courses on content creation, channel growth, monetization, and more. It's a valuable resource for both new and experienced creators.

2. Think with Google:

Provides insights and research on digital marketing trends, including YouTube. It's useful for understanding the latest industry trends and applying them to your strategy.

3. Blogs and YouTube Channels:

Follow blogs and YouTube channels dedicated to video marketing and YouTube strategies, such as VidIQ, TubeBuddy, and Roberto Blake. These resources provide tips, tutorials, and industry updates.

Equipping yourself with the right tools and resources is crucial for succeeding in YouTube marketing. From video creation and editing to SEO and analytics, these tools can help you create high-quality content, optimize for search, engage with your audience, and grow your channel. Continuously learning and adapting your strategy based on performance data and industry trends will ensure that you stay ahead in the competitive landscape of YouTube marketing. As you explore and utilize these tools, you'll be well-equipped to achieve your YouTube marketing goals and drive meaningful results for your brand.

Chapter 2: Building a Solid Foundation

Creating a successful YouTube channel begins with building a solid foundation. This chapter will guide you through the essential steps to set up your channel for success, from defining your niche and understanding your audience to creating a consistent brand identity and optimizing your channel settings. Establishing a strong foundation will ensure that your efforts in creating and promoting content are effective and sustainable in the long run.

1. Defining Your Niche

A well-defined niche is the cornerstone of a successful YouTube channel. Focusing on a specific area of interest helps you attract a dedicated audience and establish yourself as an authority in that field.

Identifying Your Interests and Expertise

- **Passion and Knowledge**: Start by listing topics you are passionate about and areas where you have significant knowledge or expertise. Your enthusiasm and understanding will translate into engaging content that resonates with viewers.
- **Market Demand**: Research popular niches and trends within the YouTube community. Tools like Google Trends, YouTube Trends, and keyword research can help identify topics with high interest and low competition.

- **Audience Needs**: Consider the problems and questions your target audience faces. Creating content that provides solutions and valuable information can help you attract a loyal following.

Evaluating Competition

- **Competitor Analysis**: Study successful channels within your potential niche. Analyze their content, engagement levels, and strategies. Identify gaps in their content that you can fill with your unique perspective.
- **Differentiation**: Think about what sets you apart from other creators. Your unique voice, style, and approach can help you stand out in a crowded market.
- **Long-term Viability**: Choose a niche that you can consistently create content for and remain interested in over the long term. Avoid overly broad or narrow niches to ensure you have enough material to sustain your channel.

2. Understanding Your Audience

Knowing your audience is crucial for creating content that resonates and engages. Understanding who your viewers are, what they like, and how they interact with your content will help you tailor your videos to meet their needs.

Demographics and Psychographics

- **Age, Gender, Location**: Use YouTube Analytics and other tools to gather demographic information about your audience. This data will help you understand the basic characteristics of your viewers.
- **Interests and Preferences**: Dive deeper into your audience's interests, hobbies, and viewing habits. Psychographic data can provide insights into their lifestyles and values, helping you create content that aligns with their interests.
- **Behavioral Data**: Analyze how your audience interacts with your content. Metrics like watch time, average view duration, and engagement rates can reveal what types of videos perform best and why.

Building Viewer Personas

- **Create Profiles**: Develop detailed profiles of your ideal viewers, including demographic and psychographic information. These personas will guide your content creation and marketing strategies.
- **Identify Pain Points**: Understand the challenges and needs of your viewer personas. Create content that addresses these pain points and offers solutions or entertainment.
- **Engage and Listen**: Interact with your audience through comments, polls, and social media. Listening to their feedback and suggestions will help you refine your content and build a stronger community.

3. Creating a Consistent Brand Identity

A strong, consistent brand identity helps you build recognition and trust with your audience. Your brand encompasses your channel's visuals, tone, and overall messaging.

Visual Branding

- **Logo and Channel Art**: Design a professional logo and channel banner that reflect your channel's theme and personality. Use consistent colors, fonts, and imagery to create a cohesive look.
- **Thumbnails**: Create eye-catching thumbnails that stand out in search results and recommendations. Use a consistent style, including colors, fonts, and layouts, to make your videos easily recognizable.
- **Video Style**: Develop a consistent visual style for your videos, including camera angles, lighting, and editing techniques. Consistency in your visuals helps reinforce your brand identity.

Tone and Voice

- **Personality**: Define the personality of your brand. Are you informative and professional, casual and friendly, or humorous and entertaining? Your personality should align with your niche and audience.
- **Language and Style**: Use a consistent tone and style in your video scripts, descriptions, and interactions with viewers. Consistency in your language helps build a strong brand voice.
- **Values and Mission**: Communicate your values and mission to your audience. This transparency helps build trust and loyalty among your viewers.

4. Optimizing Your Channel Settings

Properly setting up your channel ensures it is professional, user-friendly, and optimized for discoverability.

Channel Layout and Sections

- **Channel Trailer**: Create a compelling channel trailer that introduces new visitors to your content. Highlight what your channel is about and encourage viewers to subscribe.
- **Sections and Playlists**: Organize your videos into sections and playlists on your channel homepage. This helps viewers easily find related content and encourages binge-watching.
- **Featured Channels**: Showcase other channels you collaborate with or recommend. This can help you build connections with other creators and provide additional value to your viewers.

About Page and Links

- **About Page**: Write a clear and engaging channel description that outlines what your channel is about, what viewers can expect, and why they should subscribe. Include relevant keywords to improve searchability.
- **Contact Information**: Provide an email address or contact form for business inquiries. This makes it easy for brands and collaborators to reach out to you.

- **Social Media Links**: Include links to your social media profiles and website. This helps viewers connect with you on other platforms and learn more about your brand.

SEO and Metadata

- **Keywords**: Conduct keyword research to identify relevant terms for your niche. Use these keywords in your channel description, video titles, tags, and descriptions to improve search visibility.
- **Tags and Categories**: Use relevant tags and categories to help YouTube understand the content and context of your videos. This can improve your chances of appearing in search results and recommendations.
- **Closed Captions**: Add accurate closed captions to your videos. This not only makes your content accessible to a wider audience but also improves SEO.

Building a solid foundation is essential for long-term success on YouTube. By defining your niche, understanding your audience, creating a consistent brand identity, and optimizing your channel settings, you set the stage for creating engaging content that attracts and retains viewers. With a strong foundation in place, you'll be well-equipped to grow your channel, increase your influence, and achieve your YouTube marketing goals.

2.1 Creating a YouTube Channel: Step-by-Step Guide

Setting up a YouTube channel is the first crucial step in your journey to becoming a successful content creator. This section will provide a detailed, step-by-step guide to creating your YouTube channel, ensuring it is professional, optimized, and ready to attract viewers.

Step 1: Set Up Your Google Account

Since YouTube is a Google product, you need a Google account to create a YouTube channel. If you already have a Google account, you can use that. If not, follow these steps to create one:

1. **Go to the Google Account Creation Page:**

   - Visit the Google Account creation page (https://accounts.google.com/signup).

2. **Fill in Your Information:**

   - Enter your first and last name.
   - Choose a username for your Google account. This will also be your Gmail address.
   - Create and confirm a strong password.

3. Verify Your Account:

Follow the instructions to verify your account via phone or email.

4. Complete Your Profile:

Add a profile picture and additional information to complete your Google profile.

Step 2: Create Your YouTube Channel

Once you have a Google account, you can create your YouTube channel:

1. Sign In to YouTube:

- Go to YouTube (https://www.youtube.com) and sign in with your Google account.

2. Access YouTube Settings:

- Click on your profile picture in the top-right corner of the screen.
- Select "Your Channel" from the drop-down menu.

3. Create a New Channel:

- You will be prompted to create a channel if you don't already have one. Click on "Create Channel."
- Choose whether you want to use your name or create a custom name for your channel. For branding purposes, a custom name is usually better.

4. Channel Name and Category:

- Enter your channel name. Make sure it reflects your brand and the content you plan to create.
- Choose a category that best describes your channel (e.g., Personal, Business, etc.).

5. Customize Your Channel:

Click on "Customize Channel" to start setting up your channel's appearance and details.

Step 3: Customize Your Channel

Customizing your channel helps create a professional and inviting space for your viewers.

1. Add Channel Art:

- Channel art includes your profile picture and banner image. The banner should be 2560 x 1440 pixels and less than 6MB.
- To upload, click on the "Add channel art" button on your channel's home page and follow the instructions.

2. Channel Description:

- Click on the "About" tab on your channel page.
- Write a compelling description that explains what your channel is about, what viewers can expect, and why they should subscribe.
- Include relevant keywords to improve searchability.

3. Links and Contact Info:

- Add links to your website, social media profiles, and other relevant sites. These will appear on your banner.
- Provide an email address for business inquiries.

Step 4: Upload Your First Video

Now that your channel is set up, it's time to upload your first video.

1. Create Your Video:

- Use video creation and editing tools to produce high-quality content. Ensure your video is engaging, informative, and aligned with your channel's theme.

2. Upload Video:

- Click on the camera icon with a "+" sign in the top-right corner and select "Upload video."
- Follow the instructions to select the video file from your computer.

3. Add Video Details:

- **Title**: Create a catchy, descriptive title that includes relevant keywords.
- **Description**: Write a detailed description of your video. Include keywords and links to your website or social media profiles.
- **Tags**: Add relevant tags to help YouTube categorize and recommend your video.
- **Thumbnails**: Choose an eye-catching thumbnail. You can upload a custom thumbnail that meets YouTube's guidelines.

4. Publish Your Video:

- Choose the privacy setting (Public, Unlisted, or Private) and click "Publish" when you're ready for your video to go live.

Step 5: Optimize Your Channel Settings

Optimizing your channel settings will help improve your channel's visibility and performance.

1. **Basic Info:**

- Go to "YouTube Studio" and click on "Settings."
- Under the "Channel" section, fill in your channel's keywords, country, and other basic information.

2. **Advanced Settings:**

- Set your audience settings (e.g., whether your channel is made for kids).
- Enable features like custom URLs (once eligible) and channel recommendations.

3. **Branding:**

- Under "Customization" in YouTube Studio, you can add a watermark to your videos, usually your logo, which encourages viewers to subscribe.

4. Permissions:

- If you have a team, you can manage permissions to give different levels of access to your channel.

Step 6: Plan Your Content and Upload Schedule

Consistency is key to growing your channel. Plan your content and upload schedule to keep your audience engaged.

1. Content Calendar:

Create a content calendar to plan your video topics, filming dates, and upload times. This helps maintain a consistent posting schedule.

2. Upload Schedule:

Decide on how often you will upload videos (e.g., weekly, bi-weekly). Consistent uploads help build viewer expectations and loyalty.

3. Content Strategy:

Develop a strategy for your content, including video series, themes, and special projects. This keeps your channel dynamic and interesting.

Creating a YouTube channel is a straightforward process, but setting it up for success requires careful planning and attention to detail. By following these steps, you can establish a professional and optimized YouTube channel that is ready to attract and engage viewers. With a solid foundation in place, you can focus on creating high-quality content and growing your audience.

2.2 Defining Your Brand Identity and Voice

Creating a strong brand identity and a consistent voice is essential for standing out on YouTube and building a loyal audience. Your brand identity encompasses the visual and thematic elements that represent your channel, while your brand voice reflects your channel's personality and communication style. This section will guide you through the process of defining and developing a cohesive brand identity and voice.

Understanding Brand Identity

Your brand identity is the visual and conceptual representation of your channel. It helps viewers instantly recognize your content and understand what your channel is about.

1. **Brand Name and Logo**

- **Brand Name**: Choose a memorable name that reflects your content, and is easy to spell and search for. Your channel name should align with your niche and target audience.

- **Logo**: Design a professional logo that symbolizes your brand. Your logo should be simple, versatile, and scalable, working well across various sizes and platforms.

2. Color Scheme and Typography

- **Color Scheme**: Select a color palette that reflects your brand's personality and appeals to your audience. Consistent use of colors in your thumbnails, channel art, and videos helps establish a cohesive look.
- **Typography**: Choose fonts that are readable and reflect the tone of your brand. Use consistent fonts in your titles, thumbnails, and graphics to maintain a professional appearance.

3. Channel Art and Thumbnails

- **Channel Art**: Your channel banner is the first thing visitors see when they visit your channel. It should include your logo, tagline, and any other elements that represent your brand. Ensure it looks good on all devices.
- **Thumbnails**: Create eye-catching thumbnails that stand out and represent the content of your videos. Use consistent design elements like colors, fonts, and layouts to make your thumbnails recognizable.

4. Content Style and Visuals

- **Content Style**: Define the visual style of your videos, including camera angles, lighting, and editing techniques. Consistency in your visuals helps reinforce your brand identity.
- **Visual Elements**: Incorporate visual elements such as graphics, animations, and on-screen text that align with your brand's style.

Developing Your Brand Voice

Your brand voice is the personality and tone in which you communicate with your audience. It shapes how viewers perceive your channel and can help build a strong connection with your audience.

1. Define Your Personality

- **Brand Personality**: Determine the key traits that define your brand's personality. Are you informative and professional, casual and friendly, or humorous and entertaining? Your personality should resonate with your target audience and be authentic to you.
- **Voice Attributes**: Identify the attributes of your brand voice, such as warm, authoritative, witty, or inspirational. These attributes will guide how you communicate in your videos and other interactions.

2. Language and Tone

- **Language**: Choose language that aligns with your brand personality. Whether you use formal or informal language, jargon, or simple terms, it should be consistent and appropriate for your audience.
- **Tone**: Your tone can vary depending on the content and context, but it should always reflect your brand's voice. For example, a tutorial video might have an instructional tone, while a behind-the-scenes video might be more casual and conversational.

3. Storytelling Style

- **Narrative Approach**: Decide on your approach to storytelling. Will you use personal anecdotes, expert insights, or a mix of both? Your narrative style should engage your audience and convey your message effectively.
- **Engagement**: Use your voice to create a sense of connection with your audience. Ask questions, encourage comments, and respond to feedback to make your viewers feel involved.

4. Consistency across Platforms

- **Social Media**: Maintain a consistent voice in your social media posts, comments, and interactions. Your brand voice should be recognizable across all platforms where you engage with your audience.
- **Community Engagement**: Engage with your community in a way that reflects your brand voice. Whether responding to comments, participating in discussions, or collaborating with others, your

communication should be authentic and aligned with your brand identity.

Examples of Successful Brand Identities and Voices

- **Educational Channels**: Channels like CrashCourse use a professional yet approachable tone, combining expert knowledge with engaging visuals and a conversational style. Their consistent branding, with distinct thumbnails and a recognizable logo, reinforces their identity.
- **Lifestyle Vloggers**: Vloggers like Casey Neistat have a unique visual style and an authentic, energetic voice. His brand identity is reflected in his high-energy editing style, use of time-lapse shots, and personal storytelling approach.
- **Tech Reviewers**: Channels like Marques Brownlee (MKBHD) combine a sleek, professional visual identity with a knowledgeable and engaging voice. Consistency in thumbnails, high-quality production, and a clear, informative tone make his brand easily recognizable.

Steps to Define Your Brand Identity and Voice

- **Research and Inspiration**: Study successful channels in your niche. Identify what works well for them and what elements you can adapt for your brand.
- **Self-Assessment**: Reflect on your strengths, interests, and what makes you unique. Your brand identity and voice should be an authentic reflection of who you are.

- **Audience Insights**: Understand your target audience's preferences, values, and communication style. Your brand should resonate with their expectations and needs.
- **Develop Brand Guidelines**: Create a brand style guide that outlines your logo, color scheme, fonts, visual style, voice attributes, and tone. This guide will help maintain consistency across all your content and interactions.

Defining your brand identity and voice is a critical step in building a successful YouTube channel. A strong, consistent brand helps you stand out in a crowded market, attracts and retains viewers, and fosters a loyal community. By carefully considering your visual elements, personality, language, and engagement style, you can create a cohesive and compelling brand that resonates with your audience and supports your long-term goals.

2.3 Crafting a Compelling Channel Description and About Page

Your channel description and about page are crucial elements that help new visitors understand what your channel is about, why they should subscribe, and what they can expect from your content. A well-crafted description can enhance your channel's visibility, attract the right audience, and encourage engagement. This section will guide you through creating an engaging and informative channel description and about page.

Importance of a Strong Channel Description

Your channel description serves several key purposes:

- **First Impressions**: It's often the first thing potential subscribers read when they visit your channel. A clear and compelling description can make a positive first impression and entice viewers to explore your content.
- **SEO Optimization**: Including relevant keywords in your description helps improve your channel's visibility in search results, making it easier for viewers to find your content.
- **Audience Understanding**: It provides an overview of your channel's focus, content type, and posting schedule, helping viewers decide if your channel aligns with their interests.

Crafting Your Channel Description

1. Start with a Hook

- Begin with a catchy opening line that grabs attention. This could be a unique selling proposition, a provocative question, or a bold statement that encapsulates your channel's essence.
- Example: "Ready to unlock your creative potential? Welcome to [Your Channel Name], where we transform every day ideas into extraordinary projects!"

2. Introduce Yourself and Your Channel

- Briefly introduce yourself and explain what your channel is about. Mention your niche, the type of content you create, and the value you provide to your audience.
- Example: "I'm [Your Name], a passionate DIY enthusiast who loves sharing innovative projects, tips, and tutorials. On this channel, you'll find everything from home decor hacks to upcycling ideas."

3. Highlight the Benefits for Viewers

- Clearly state what viewers will gain from subscribing to your channel. Focus on the benefits and outcomes they can expect.
- Example: "Join our community to discover step-by-step guides, creative inspiration, and practical tips to bring your DIY dreams to life. Whether you're a beginner or a seasoned crafter, there's something here for everyone."

4. Include Your Upload Schedule

- Inform your viewers about your posting frequency to set expectations. Consistency in uploading helps build a loyal audience.
- Example: "New videos every Wednesday and Saturday, so hit that subscribe button and never miss an update!"

5. Call to Action

- Encourage viewers to take action, such as subscribing to your channel, watching specific videos, or following you on social media.
- Example: "Don't forget to subscribe and click the bell icon to get notified whenever I upload new content. Let's get creative together!"

6. Incorporate Keywords Naturally

- Use relevant keywords throughout your description to improve search visibility. However, avoid keyword stuffing; the text should read naturally and be engaging.
- Example: "DIY projects, home decor tips, creative tutorials, crafting ideas, and more!"

Crafting Your About Page

The About page provides additional details about your channel, its purpose, and the creator behind it. Here's how to make it effective:

1. Detailed Introduction

- Expand on your channel description with more details about your background, expertise, and the inspiration behind your channel.

- Example: "I'm [Your Name], and my passion for DIY started when I was a kid, building treehouses and crafting gifts for friends. With years of experience and a love for creativity, I started this channel to share my knowledge and inspire others to embrace DIY."

2. Mission and Vision

- Clearly state your channel's mission and vision. What do you hope to achieve with your content, and how do you want to impact your audience?
- Example: "My mission is to make DIY accessible and enjoyable for everyone. I believe that creativity is for everyone, and with the right guidance, anyone can create beautiful, functional projects."

3. Content Overview

- Provide a detailed overview of the types of content you produce. Mention any special series or recurring themes.
- Example: "On this channel, you'll find a variety of content including home decor projects, upcycling tutorials, seasonal crafts, and DIY challenges. Check out our popular series 'Weekend Projects' for quick and fun ideas you can complete in just a few hours."

4. Community Engagement

- Highlight your community's involvement and how you engage with your audience. Encourage viewers to join the conversation.
- Example: "Our community is at the heart of everything we do. I love hearing from you, so leave your comments, suggestions, and project requests. Let's learn and grow together!"

5. Contact Information

- Provide an email address for business inquiries and collaboration opportunities. You can also include links to your social media profiles.
- Example: "For business inquiries, please contact me at [your email address]. Follow me on Instagram, Facebook, and Twitter for behind-the-scenes content and more DIY inspiration."

6. Legal and Disclosure Information

- Include any necessary legal disclaimers or disclosure information, especially if you engage in sponsorships or affiliate marketing.
- Example: "Some of the links in my videos and on this page are affiliate links, meaning I may earn a commission if you purchase them. This helps support the channel at no extra cost to you."

By clearly communicating what your channel is about, highlighting the benefits for viewers, and providing a personal touch, you can create a strong first impression and build a loyal audience. Use these guidelines to craft descriptions that are engaging, informative, and optimized for discoverability, setting the stage for your channel's growth and success.

2.4 Designing Eye-Catching Channel Art and Thumbnails

Your channel art and thumbnails are the visual cornerstones of your YouTube presence. They serve as the first impression for potential viewers and play a crucial role in attracting clicks and subscriptions. This section will guide you through the principles and techniques for designing compelling channel art and thumbnails that stand out and drive engagement.

The Importance of Visual Appeal

Visual appeal is critical on YouTube, where competition for attention is fierce. High-quality channel art and thumbnails can:

- **Attract Attention**: Eye-catching visuals stand out in search results and the YouTube homepage, increasing the likelihood of viewers clicking on your content.
- **Establish Brand Identity**: Consistent and well-designed visuals reinforce your brand identity, making your channel more recognizable.
- **Convey Professionalism**: Quality graphics convey that you are serious about your content, which can build trust with potential subscribers.

Designing Channel Art

Channel art includes your channel banner, profile picture, and other graphical elements that define your channel's visual identity.

1. Channel Banner

Size and Dimensions: The recommended size for YouTube channel banners is 2560 x 1440 pixels, with a safe area of 1546 x 423 pixels for text and logos. This ensures your banner looks good on all devices.

Key Elements:

- **Logo**: Incorporate your logo to reinforce brand recognition.
- **Channel Name**: Make sure your channel name is visible.
- **Tagline**: If you have a tagline, include it to quickly convey what your channel is about.
- **Upload Schedule**: Mention your upload schedule if you have one to set expectations.
- **Social Media Links**: Include icons or links to your social media profiles.

Design Tips:

- **Simplicity**: Keep the design clean and uncluttered. Avoid overloading with too much text or too many elements.
- **Consistency**: Use colors, fonts, and imagery consistent with your overall brand identity.
- **High-Quality Images**: Use high-resolution images to ensure your banner looks sharp on all devices.

Profile Picture

Size and Dimensions: The recommended size for YouTube profile pictures is 800 x 800 pixels. Ensure the image looks good as a small icon since it appears next to your video titles and comments.

Key Elements:

- **Logo or Headshot**: Use a clear, recognizable image, such as your logo or a professional headshot.
- **Visibility**: Make sure the image is easy to see and understand even at small sizes.

Designing Thumbnails

Thumbnails are miniature representations of your videos and are one of the most critical factors in driving clicks.

Thumbnail Dimensions

- **Size and Dimensions**: The optimal size for YouTube thumbnails is 1280 x 720 pixels, with a minimum width of 640 pixels. Maintain a 16:9 aspect ratio.

Key Elements of Effective Thumbnails

1. Bold, Readable Text:

- **Font Choice**: Use bold, easy-to-read fonts. Avoid overly decorative fonts that are hard to read at a glance.
- **Text Placement**: Position text strategically, ensuring it doesn't obscure important visual elements.

2. High-Quality Images:

- **Resolution**: Use high-resolution images to ensure your thumbnails look sharp on all devices.
- **Clarity**: Choose images that are clear and not too cluttered. The subject should be easily identifiable.

3. Brand Consistency:

- **Color Scheme**: Use a consistent color scheme that aligns with your brand. This helps create a cohesive look across all your thumbnails.
- **Logo**: Include a small logo or branding element on each thumbnail for recognition.

4. Design Tips for Thumbnails

- **Focus on Faces**: Thumbnails with human faces, especially with expressive emotions, tend to attract more clicks. Faces help create a connection with viewers.
- **Contrast and Brightness**: Use high contrast and bright colors to make your thumbnail stand out. Ensure the main elements are well-lit and distinguishable.
- **Action and Energy**: Depict action or dynamic scenes to convey energy and excitement. Thumbnails that promise engaging content tend to perform better.
- **Tease the Content**: Create intrigue by hinting at the content without giving everything away. Use visual cues to make viewers curious.

Tools for Creating Channel Art and Thumbnails

1. Graphic Design Software:

- **Adobe Photoshop**: A powerful tool for creating detailed and high-quality graphics. Ideal for those with some design experience.
- **Canva**: User-friendly with many templates specifically for YouTube banners and thumbnails. Great for beginners and quick designs.
- **GIMP**: A free, open-source alternative to Photoshop with robust features for creating and editing images.

2. Thumbnail-Specific Tools:

- **TubeBuddy**: Offers a thumbnail generator along with other YouTube optimization tools.
- **Snappa**: Provides easy-to-use templates for creating professional-looking thumbnails quickly.

Steps to Create Effective Channel Art and Thumbnails

1. **Plan Your Design:**

Sketch out your ideas or use a storyboard to visualize how your elements will fit together.

Think about your audience and what visuals will appeal to them.

2. **Use Templates:**

Utilize templates from Canva, Adobe Spark, or other tools to speed up the design process and ensure proper dimensions.

3. **Test and Iterate:**

A/B tests different thumbnail designs to see which ones perform better.

Analyze your click-through rates and adjust your designs based on performance data.

4. Seek Feedback:

Ask for feedback from your audience or peers. Constructive criticism can help improve your designs.

Designing eye-catching channel art and thumbnails is essential for attracting viewers and building your brand on YouTube. By focusing on visual appeal, consistency, and clarity, you can create compelling graphics that draw attention and encourage viewers to engage with your content. Use the tools and tips provided in this section to elevate your channel's visual presentation and make a lasting impression on your audience.

2.5 Setting up Your Channel for Success: Playlists, Tags, and Categories

Effectively organizing and categorizing your content is crucial for maximizing your channel's potential and ensuring viewers can easily find and engage with your videos. This section will cover how to set up playlists, tags, and categories to enhance your channel's discoverability, user experience, and overall success.

Playlists: Curating Your Content

Playlists are a powerful tool for organizing your videos into logical, viewer-friendly collections. They help keep viewers on your channel longer by automatically playing the next video in the list, enhancing watch time and viewer retention.

1. Creating Playlists

- Identify Themes: Group your videos by themes, topics, or series. For example, if you run a cooking channel, you might have playlists for "Quick Recipes," "Healthy Meals," and "Desserts."
- New Playlist Setup:

  I. Go to YouTube Studio.
  II. Click on "Playlists" in the left-hand menu.
  III. Click "New Playlist."
  IV. Enter a title and choose the privacy setting (Public, Unlisted, or Private).
  V. Click "Create."

Optimizing Playlists

- **Titles and Descriptions**: Use descriptive titles and keyword-rich descriptions. This helps with SEO and gives viewers a clear idea of what to expect.
- **Ordering Videos**: Arrange videos in a logical sequence that makes sense to the viewer. For example, in a tutorial series, order the videos from beginner to advanced.
- **Featured Playlists**: Highlight important playlists on your channel's homepage to guide viewers to your best or most popular content.

Benefits of Playlists

- **Increased Watch Time**: Playlists can automatically play the next video, keeping viewers engaged longer.
- **Improved Discoverability**: Playlists appear in search results and can be found in the "Related Videos" section on YouTube.
- **Better User Experience**: Playlists help viewers easily find content that interests them without needing to search through your entire video library.

Tags: Boosting Your Video's Reach

Tags are keywords you add to your videos to help YouTube understand the content and context of your videos. They play a crucial role in video SEO and can significantly impact your discoverability.

1. Choosing Effective Tags

- **Relevance**: Ensure your tags are directly related to your video content. Misleading tags can harm your channel's reputation and performance.
- **Specific and Broad Tags**: Use a mix of specific tags (e.g., "chocolate cake recipe") and broad tags (e.g., "baking") to reach a wider audience.
- **Long-Tail Keywords**: Include long-tail keywords that viewers might search for, such as "how to bake a chocolate cake."

2. Best Practices for Tags

- **Primary Keywords**: Start with your primary keywords, which should be included in your title and description.
- **Secondary Keywords**: Add secondary keywords that are related to your primary keywords.
- **Competitor Analysis**: Look at tags used by successful channels in your niche to find additional relevant keywords.

3. How to Add Tags

- **During Upload:**

    I.   When uploading a video, go to the "Details" tab.
    II. Scroll down to the "Tags" section.
    III. Enter your tags separated by commas.

- **After Upload:**

    I.   Go to YouTube Studio.
    II. Click on "Videos" in the left-hand menu.
    III. Select the video you want to add tags to and click "Edit."
    IV. Enter your tags in the "Tags" section and save changes.

Categories: Aligning Your Content with Viewer Interests

Categories help YouTube understand the context of your videos and recommend them to the right audience. Selecting the appropriate category is essential for improving the reach and relevance of your content.

1. Available Categories

- YouTube offers several categories, such as Education, Entertainment, Gaming, How-to & Style, and more. Choose the one that best fits your content.

2. Choosing the Right Category

- **Content-Type**: Align your category choice with the type of content you produce. For example, if you create tutorials, "How-to & Style" might be the best fit.
- **Target Audience**: Consider the interests of your target audience. A vlogging channel might fit into "People & Blogs," while a tech review channel might belong in "Science & Technology."

3. Setting Your Category

- **During Upload:**

I. When uploading a video, go to the "Details" tab.
II. Scroll down to the "Category" section.
III. Select the appropriate category from the dropdown menu.

- **After Upload:**

I. Go to YouTube Studio.
II. Click on "Videos" in the left-hand menu.
III. Select the video you want to categorize and click "Edit."
IV. Choose the appropriate category from the dropdown menu and save changes.

Integrating Playlists, Tags, and Categories

For optimal performance and user experience, it's important to integrate your playlists, tags, and categories seamlessly.

- **Cross-Promotion**: Use video descriptions and end screens to promote related playlists. This encourages viewers to watch more of your content.
- **Consistent Tagging**: Use consistent tagging across your videos to create a network of related content, making it easier for YouTube to recommend your videos.
- **Categorical Alignment**: Ensure that your videos are consistently categorized to help YouTube understand your niche and target audience better.

Monitoring and Adjusting

Regularly review your analytics to understand how your playlists, tags, and categories are performing. Use this data to make informed adjustments.

- **YouTube Analytics**: Monitor metrics such as watch time, click-through rates, and audience retention to evaluate the effectiveness of your playlists and tags.
- **Adjusting Strategies**: If certain tags or categories are underperforming, experiment with different keywords and categories to see what resonates more with your audience.
- **Feedback Loop**: Pay attention to viewer feedback in comments and use this to refine your content organization strategy.

Effectively setting up your channel with well-organized playlists, strategic tags, and appropriate categories is essential for enhancing discoverability, engagement, and viewer satisfaction. By following the best practices outlined in this section, you can create a streamlined, user-friendly channel that attracts and retains viewers, ultimately setting your channel up for long-term success.

Chapter 3: Content Creation Strategies

Content creation is both an art and a science, a delicate dance between creativity and analytics. Whether you are a seasoned marketer, an aspiring influencer, or a small business owner, mastering content creation is essential for building a meaningful connection with your audience. This chapter delves into the strategies that can transform your content from ordinary to extraordinary.

The Foundation: Understanding Your Audience

Before diving into the nitty-gritty of content creation, it's crucial to understand who you're creating content for. Knowing your audience is the cornerstone of any successful content strategy. Without this understanding, your efforts may fall flat, no matter how well-crafted your content is.

Creating Audience Personas

Start by developing detailed audience personas. These are semi-fictional characters that represent your ideal customers. To create these personas, gather data through surveys, interviews, and analytics. Consider factors such as:

- **Demographics**: Age, gender, income, education level, and location.
- **Psychographics**: Interests, hobbies, values, and lifestyle.

- **Behavioral Insights**: Purchase behavior, online activity, and brand loyalty.

Once you have this data, create 3-5 personas that encapsulate the different segments of your audience. Give them names, backstories, and even photos to bring them to life. This practice helps you empathize with your audience and tailor your content to meet their needs and preferences.

Crafting Compelling Stories

At the heart of any great content is a compelling story. Stories have the power to evoke emotions, create connections, and drive action. Here's how to craft stories that resonate with your audience:

The Hero's Journey

One of the most effective storytelling frameworks is the Hero's Journey, a narrative structure identified by Joseph Campbell. This framework involves a hero who embarks on an adventure, faces challenges, and ultimately triumphs. Here's how you can apply this to your content:

1. **The Ordinary World**: Introduce the status quo and the hero (your audience or customer).
2. **The Call to Adventure**: Present a problem or challenge that disrupts the status quo.

3. **Crossing the Threshold**: Show the hero taking the first steps towards solving the problem.
4. **The Trials**: Highlight the obstacles and difficulties the hero faces.
5. **The Victory**: Celebrate the hero's success and the resolution of the problem.
6. **The Return**: Reinforce the transformation and lessons learned.

By positioning your audience as the hero and your product or service as the guide, you create a narrative that is both engaging and relatable.

The Power of Visual Content

Visual content is a potent tool in your content arsenal. Humans are inherently visual creatures, and images, videos, and infographics can convey messages more effectively than text alone.

Types of Visual Content

- **Images**: Use high-quality photos and graphics to break up text and add visual interest. Tools like Canva can help you create stunning visuals even if you're not a designer.
- **Videos**: From short social media clips to in-depth tutorials, videos can engage your audience on a deeper level. Platforms like YouTube, Instagram, and TikTok are perfect for video content.
- **Infographics**: These are great for presenting complex information in an easy-to-digest format. Infographics are particularly effective for sharing statistics, processes, and timelines.

Best Practices for Visual Content

- **Consistency**: Maintain a consistent style and color scheme to reinforce your brand identity.
- **Relevance**: Ensure your visuals support and enhance the message you're conveying.
- **Accessibility**: Use alt text for images and subtitles for videos to make your content accessible to all users.

Leveraging User-Generated Content

User-generated content (UGC) is a powerful way to build community and trust. UGC includes any content created by your audience, such as reviews, testimonials, social media posts, and more.

Encouraging UGC

- **Create Hashtags**: Develop unique hashtags that your audience can use when sharing content related to your brand.
- **Run Contests**: Host contests that encourage your followers to create and share content. Offer prizes that are appealing and relevant to your audience.
- **Feature UGC**: Showcase user-generated content on your website, social media channels, and marketing materials. This not only provides social proof but also motivates others to contribute.

Benefits of UGC

- **Authenticity**: UGC is perceived as more genuine and trustworthy than branded content.
- **Engagement**: It fosters a sense of community and encourages interaction with your brand.
- **Cost-Effectiveness**: It provides you with valuable content without significant investment.

Optimizing for SEO

Search engine optimization (SEO) is critical for ensuring your content reaches a broader audience. Effective SEO involves optimizing your content so that it ranks higher in search engine results pages (SERPs).

Keyword Research

Start with thorough keyword research to understand what terms your audience is searching for. Tools like Google Keyword Planner, Ahrefs, and SEMrush can help identify relevant keywords. Focus on both high-volume keywords and long-tail keywords (more specific phrases that are less competitive).

On-Page SEO

- **Title Tags**: Include your primary keyword in the title tag, and keep it under 60 characters.
- **Meta Descriptions**: Write compelling meta descriptions that include your target keywords and entice users to click. Aim for 150-160 characters.
- **Headings**: Use H1 tags for titles and H2, and H3 tags for subheadings to structure your content. Incorporate keywords naturally.
- **Content Quality**: Write comprehensive, high-quality content that provides value. Google favors in-depth articles that thoroughly cover a topic.
- **Internal Linking**: Link to other relevant pages on your site to improve navigation and keep users engaged.

Off-Page SEO

- **Backlinks**: Earn backlinks from reputable websites to increase your content's authority. This can be achieved through guest posting, collaborations, and creating shareable content.
- **Social Signals**: While social media shares do not directly impact SEO, they can drive traffic to your site, which can improve your rankings.

Measuring Success

To refine your content strategy, you need to measure its effectiveness. Use analytics tools like Google Analytics, social media insights, and content management system (CMS) analytics to track performance.

Key Metrics to Monitor

- **Traffic**: Monitor the number of visitors to your content.
- **Engagement**: Track likes, shares, comments, and time spent on the page.
- **Conversions**: Measure how well your content drives desired actions, such as sign-ups, purchases, or downloads.
- **Bounce Rate**: High bounce rates may indicate that your content isn't meeting audience expectations.

Regularly review these metrics to identify what's working and what needs improvement. Use this data to tweak your strategy and continuously enhance your content.

Mastering content creation is a journey that requires a deep understanding of your audience, a flair for storytelling, a knack for visual design, and a strategic approach to SEO. By leveraging these content creation strategies, you can craft content that not only captivates but also drives meaningful engagement and results. As you refine your skills and adapt to the ever-changing digital landscape, you'll find that the art of content creation is a powerful tool for connecting with your audience and achieving your goals.

3.1 Identifying Your Target Audience

Understanding your target audience is the linchpin of an effective content strategy. Without a clear picture of who your audience is, your content may miss the mark, leading to wasted resources and missed opportunities. Here, we'll explore the steps and techniques to accurately identify and understand your target audience in detail.

Step 1: Collecting Demographic Data

The first step in identifying your target audience is gathering demographic data. This includes basic information such as age, gender, income, education level, and geographic location. There are several ways to collect this data:

- **Website Analytics**: Tools like Google Analytics provide insights into the demographic makeup of your website visitors. You can see details like age distribution, gender split, and geographic locations.
- **Social Media Insights**: Platforms like Facebook, Instagram, and LinkedIn offer analytics that show who is engaging with your content.
- **Customer Surveys**: Directly asking your audience through surveys can yield valuable demographic data. Tools like SurveyMonkey or Google Forms can facilitate this process.

Step 2: Understanding Psychographics

Beyond demographics, psychographics delve into the psychological attributes of your audience. This includes their interests, values, attitudes, and lifestyles. Psychographic data helps you understand why your audience behaves the way they do, which is crucial for creating content that resonates on a deeper level.

- **Interests and Hobbies**: What are your audience's passions and interests? This can influence the type of content they find engaging.

- **Values and Beliefs**: Understanding the core values and beliefs of your audience can guide the tone and messaging of your content.
- **Lifestyle**: Consider factors like their daily routines, media consumption habits, and social behaviors.

You can gather psychographic data through customer surveys, interviews, and even by analyzing the content your audience engages with on social media.

Step 3: Analyzing Behavioral Insights

Behavioral insights provide information on how your audience interacts with your brand and content. This includes their purchasing behavior, online activity, and engagement patterns. Key behavioral data points include:

- **Purchase History**: What products or services are they buying? How often do they make purchases?
- **Website Behavior**: Use tools like Google Analytics to track how visitors navigate your site. Pay attention to metrics like time on the page, bounce rate, and conversion paths.
- **Engagement Metrics**: On social media, track likes, shares, comments, and click-through rates to see what type of content performs best.

Behavioral data helps you identify patterns and preferences, allowing you to tailor your content to better meet the needs and expectations of your audience.

Step 4: Creating Audience Personas

With demographic, psychographic, and behavioral data in hand, you can create detailed audience personas. These personas are fictional representations of your ideal customers, each embodying a distinct segment of your audience.

- **Persona Details**: Give each persona a name, age, occupation, and backstory. Include key demographic, psychographic, and behavioral characteristics.
- **Pain Points and Needs**: Identify the specific challenges and needs of each persona. This helps in creating content that addresses their problems and offers solutions.
- **Content Preferences**: Outline what type of content each persona prefers. Do they like in-depth articles, short blog posts, videos, or infographics?

Creating personas helps you humanize your audience and fosters a deeper understanding of their needs and preferences.

Step 5: Continuous Refinement

Identifying your target audience is not a one-time task. It requires continuous refinement as your audience evolves and new data becomes available. Regularly revisit and update your personas based on fresh insights and changing trends.

- **Monitor Trends**: Stay updated with industry trends and how they might impact your audience.
- **Feedback Loops**: Encourage feedback from your audience through comments, surveys, and direct interactions. Use this feedback to refine your understanding.
- **Data Analysis**: Continuously analyze your performance metrics to see if your content is hitting the mark with your target audience.

By following these steps and regularly refining your approach, you can develop a nuanced understanding of your target audience, enabling you to create content that truly resonates and drives engagement.

3.2 Planning and Scripting Engaging Videos

Video content has become a powerhouse in the digital landscape, offering a dynamic and engaging way to connect with your audience. However, creating compelling videos requires careful planning and scripting to ensure they resonate with viewers and drive meaningful engagement. In this section, we'll explore the steps involved in planning and scripting engaging videos.

Step 1: Define Your Objective

Before diving into video production, clarify the objective of your video. What do you want to achieve? Whether it's raising brand awareness, driving sales, or educating your audience, having a clear goal will inform the content and tone of your video.

Example Objectives:

- Introduce a new product or service
- Showcase customer testimonials
- Demonstrate how to use your product
- Share industry insights or thought leadership

Step 2: Know Your Audience

Understanding your audience is key to creating videos that resonate with them. Refer back to the audience personas created in Chapter 3.1 to ensure your video content aligns with their interests, preferences, and pain points.

Audience Considerations:

- What topics are they interested in?
- What tone and style of video do they prefer?
- What challenges are they facing that your video can address?

Step 3: Brainstorm Content Ideas

Once you know your objective and audience, brainstorm content ideas that will captivate and engage viewers. Consider the format, style, and approach that best fits your objectives and resonates with your audience.

Content Ideas:

- Product demonstrations or tutorials
- Behind-the-scenes glimpses of your business
- Q&A sessions with industry experts
- Customer success stories or testimonials

Step 4: Develop a Script

A well-crafted script is the backbone of any engaging video. It provides structure, ensures clarity, and helps convey your message effectively. When scripting your video, keep these tips in mind:

- **Start with a Hook**: Capture viewers' attention from the start with a compelling hook that addresses their interests or pain points.
- **Keep it Concise**: Attention spans are short, so keep your script concise and to the point. Aim for clarity and avoid unnecessary fluff.
- **Tell a Story**: Weave a narrative that engages viewers emotionally and keeps them invested in your message.
- **Include a Call to Action (CTA)**: Prompt viewers to take action, whether it's visiting your website, subscribing to your channel, or making a purchase.

Step 5: Plan Visuals and B-Roll

In addition to the script, plan out the visuals and B-roll footage that will accompany your video. Visuals play a crucial role in keeping viewers engaged and reinforcing your message.

- **Storyboarding**: Sketch out a storyboard that outlines the visual sequence of your video, including shots, transitions, and graphics.
- **Location and Set Design**: Choose appropriate locations or set designs that complement your message and align with your brand.
- **B-Roll Footage**: Gather supplementary footage to enhance your main content, such as close-ups, action shots, or scenes that illustrate key points.

Step 6: Rehearse and refine

Before filming, rehearse your script and refine any areas that feel awkward or unclear. Practice delivering your lines naturally and with confidence. Consider enlisting feedback from colleagues or friends to fine-tune your delivery.

Step 7: Filming and Editing

Once you're confident in your script and performance, it's time to film your video. Pay attention to lighting, sound quality, and camera angles to ensure professional production values. After filming, edit your footage to polish the final product, adding music, graphics, and transitions as needed.

Step 8: Optimize for Distribution

Finally, optimize your video for distribution across various platforms. Consider aspects like video length, aspect ratio, and captions to maximize reach and engagement on platforms like YouTube, Facebook, Instagram, and LinkedIn.

By following these steps and putting thought into planning and scripting, you can create engaging videos that resonate with your audience, drive meaningful engagement, and achieve your objectives.

3.3 Production Tips: Lighting, Sound, and Camera Work

Effective video production relies on more than just a compelling script and engaging content. Factors like lighting, sound quality, and camera work play a crucial role in creating professional-looking videos that captivate viewers and convey your message effectively. In this section, we'll explore some essential production tips to elevate the quality of your videos.

Lighting

Good lighting is essential for creating visually appealing videos that look polished and professional. Here are some lighting tips to consider:

- **Natural Light**: Whenever possible, utilize natural light as your primary light source. Position yourself or your subject near a window to take advantage of soft, diffused natural light.

- **Three-Point Lighting**: Use a three-point lighting setup consisting of a key light, fill light, and backlight. This setup helps balance shadows and highlights, creating depth and dimension in your shots.
- **Avoid Harsh Shadows**: Harsh shadows can be distracting and unflattering. Diffuse light sources using softboxes, umbrellas, or diffusion panels to create soft, even lighting.
- **Consider Color Temperature**: Pay attention to the color temperature of your lights to ensure consistency. Match your lighting setup to the ambient lighting conditions to maintain a natural look.

Sound

Poor audio quality can undermine even the most visually stunning video. Here are some sound tips to ensure clear, crisp audio:

- **Use External Microphones**: Invest in high-quality external microphones for better sound capture. Options include lavalier (lapel) mics for individual speakers and shotgun mics for capturing audio from a distance.
- **Minimize Background Noise**: Choose quiet shooting locations to minimize background noise. Use soundproofing materials or blankets to dampen echoes and reverberations.
- **Monitor Audio Levels**: Keep an eye on audio levels during recording to avoid clipping or distortion. Aim for clear, balanced audio without peaking into the red.

- **Consider Voiceovers**: If recording audio on location isn't feasible, consider recording voiceovers separately in a controlled environment for better clarity and consistency.

Camera Work

Effective camera work can enhance the visual impact of your videos and keep viewers engaged. Here are some camera tips to consider:

- **Stabilize Your Shots**: Use tripods, gimbals, or stabilizers to keep your shots steady and smooth. Avoid shaky footage, which can be distracting and amateurish.
- **Experiment with Angles and Perspectives**: Get creative with your camera angles and perspectives to add visual interest. Use low angles for a sense of drama or high angles for an aerial view.
- **Focus on Composition**: Pay attention to composition principles like the rule of thirds, leading lines, and framing to create visually pleasing shots. Experiment with different compositions to find what works best for your subject.
- **Adjust Camera Settings**: Familiarize yourself with your camera's settings and adjust them as needed for optimal exposure, focus, and white balance. Shoot in the highest resolution and frame rate possible for maximum quality.

Post-Production

Once you've captured your footage, post-production is where you bring it all together. Here are some post-production tips to consider:

- **Editing**: Use video editing software to trim footage, add transitions, insert graphics, and enhance colors. Aim for a cohesive visual style that aligns with your brand.
- **Color Grading**: Enhance the look of your footage through color grading, adjusting contrast, saturation, and color temperature to achieve the desired mood or tone.
- **Audio Mixing**: Balance audio levels, remove background noise, and add music or sound effects to enhance the overall audio experience.
- **Optimize for Distribution**: Consider the platform where your video will be shared and optimize it accordingly. Adjust aspect ratio, resolution, and file format for optimal viewing on different devices and platforms.

By paying attention to lighting, sound, and camera work, both during production and post-production, and you can elevate the quality of your videos and create content that captivates and engages your audience.

3.4 Editing Like a Pro: Software and Techniques

Video editing is where the magic happens. It's where raw footage transforms into polished, engaging content that captivates viewers and conveys your message effectively. In this section, we'll explore the software tools and editing techniques you need to edit like a pro.

Editing Software

Choosing the right editing software is crucial for a smooth and efficient editing process. Here are some popular options:

- **Adobe Premiere Pro**: A professional-grade editing software favored by filmmakers, YouTubers, and content creators. It offers a wide range of advanced features and integrations with other Adobe Creative Cloud applications.
- **Final Cut Pro X**: Apple's flagship video editing software, known for its intuitive interface and powerful editing tools. It's popular among Mac users and offers features like magnetic timeline and multi-cam editing.
- **DaVinci Resolve**: A comprehensive editing and color grading software used by professional editors and colorists. It offers advanced features for both editing and color correction, making it a versatile choice for post-production workflows.
- **iMovie**: A beginner-friendly editing software available for Mac and iOS devices. It offers basic editing tools and templates, making it ideal for simple video projects or beginners learning the ropes of editing.

Editing Techniques

Once you've chosen your editing software, it's time to dive into editing techniques that will help you create professional-looking videos:

- **Cutting and Trimming**: Use the razor tool or shortcut keys to cut and trim your footage, removing unwanted sections and tightening up the pacing of your video.
- **Transitions**: Experiment with different transition effects to smooth out cuts between clips and add visual interest. Avoid overusing flashy transitions, and opt for simple cuts or fades for a more professional look.

- **Color Correction**: Use color correction tools to adjust the exposure, contrast, saturation, and white balance of your footage. Aim for a consistent look and feel throughout your video, and use color grading to enhance the mood or tone.
- **Audio Mixing**: Balance audio levels, remove background noise, and add music or sound effects to enhance the overall audio experience. Use keyframes to adjust volume levels dynamically and create smooth transitions between audio clips.
- **Titles and Graphics**: Incorporate titles, lower thirds, and graphics to add context, information, and branding to your video. Use animation presets or create custom animations to make your titles more dynamic and engaging.
- **Effects and Filters**: Experiment with effects and filters to add visual flair to your video. Use effects like blurs, glows, and stylized filters to enhance certain scenes or evoke a specific mood.

Workflow Tips

To streamline your editing process and work more efficiently, consider the following workflow tips:

- **Organize Your Footage**: Organize your footage into bins or folders based on categories, scenes, or types of shots. This makes it easier to find and access the clips you need during editing.
- **Create Proxy Files**: If you're working with high-resolution footage, create proxy files to speed up your editing workflow. Proxy files are lower-resolution versions of your footage that are easier to edit and playback.

- **Use Keyboard Shortcuts**: Learn and use keyboard shortcuts to speed up repetitive tasks and navigate your editing software more efficiently. Customize shortcuts to suit your editing style and preferences.
- **Save Regularly**: Save your project frequently to avoid losing progress in case of a software crash or technical issue. Consider enabling auto-save features or setting up backups for added peace of mind.

By mastering editing software and techniques, you can transform your raw footage into polished, professional-looking videos that captivate and engage your audience. Experiment with different tools and effects, and don't be afraid to let your creativity shine through in your edits.

3.5 Leveraging Trends and Viral Content Opportunities

In the fast-paced world of digital media, staying ahead of trends and tapping into viral content opportunities can significantly boost your reach and engagement. In this section, we'll explore strategies for leveraging trends and capitalizing on viral content to amplify your online presence.

Monitoring Trends

Keeping a pulse on current trends is essential for identifying opportunities to create timely and relevant content. Here are some effective ways to monitor trends:

- **Social Media Platforms**: Follow trending hashtags, topics, and discussions on platforms like Twitter, Instagram, and TikTok. Pay attention to what's trending in your industry and among your target audience.
- **Google Trends**: Use Google Trends to track the popularity of search queries over time. Explore trending topics and related searches to uncover content ideas that are gaining traction.
- **Industry News and Publications**: Stay informed about industry news, events, and developments that may spark interest among your audience. Subscribe to relevant publications, newsletters, and blogs for insights into emerging trends.

Capitalizing on Viral Content

Viral content has the power to reach massive audiences and generate significant engagement in a short period. Here's how to capitalize on viral content opportunities:

- **Embrace Creativity**: Think outside the box and experiment with unconventional ideas and formats. Viral content often thrives on novelty and creativity, so don't be afraid to take risks and push boundaries.
- **Tap into Emotions**: Emotional content tends to resonate with audiences and has a higher likelihood of going viral. Whether it's humor, inspiration, or nostalgia, evoke emotions that connect with your audience on a personal level.
- **Engage with Trends**: Keep an eye on emerging trends and capitalize on them by creating relevant content. Incorporate

trending topics, challenges, or memes into your content to ride the wave of virality.

- **Collaborate with Influencers**: Partnering with influencers who have a large and engaged following can amplify the reach of your content. Collaborate on creative projects or campaigns that align with both your brand and the influencer's audience.

Creating Shareable Content

To maximize the virality of your content, focus on creating shareable content that encourages audience engagement and sharing. Here are some tips for creating shareable content:

- **Keep it Concise**: Capture attention quickly and deliver your message concisely. Short-form content performs well on social media platforms where attention spans are short.
- **Add Value**: Provide value to your audience through informative, entertaining, or inspirational content. Share practical tips, insights, or behind-the-scenes glimpses that resonate with your audience's interests.
- **Include a Call to Action (CTA)**: Encourage viewers to engage with your content by including a clear call to action. Whether it's liking, commenting, sharing, or visiting your website, prompt viewers to take action to amplify the reach of your content.
- **Optimize for Mobile**: With the majority of internet users accessing content on mobile devices, ensure your content is optimized for mobile viewing. Use mobile-friendly formats, aspect ratios, and captions to enhance accessibility and engagement.

Analyzing Performance

Track the performance of your content to identify what resonates with your audience and inform future strategies. Pay attention to metrics like engagement, shares, reach, and conversions to gauge the effectiveness of your efforts.

- **A/B Testing**: Experiment with different content formats, styles, and messaging to see what resonates best with your audience. Use A/B testing to compare the performance of different variations and optimize your approach accordingly.
- **Iterate and Improve**: Continuously iterate on your content strategy based on performance data and audience feedback. Learn from successes and failures to refine your approach and stay ahead of evolving trends.

By staying attuned to trends, capitalizing on viral content opportunities, and creating shareable content that resonates with your audience, you can amplify your online presence and drive meaningful engagement with your brand. Keep experimenting, learning, and adapting to stay ahead in the ever-changing digital landscape.

Chapter 4: Optimizing for Search and Discovery

In the vast digital landscape, where countless websites compete for attention, mastering the art of search engine optimization (SEO) is essential for ensuring your content stands out and reaches its intended audience. This chapter delves into the strategies and techniques for optimizing your content to improve search visibility and discovery.

Understanding Search Engine Optimization (SEO)

SEO is the process of optimizing your website and content to rank higher in search engine results pages (SERPs) and attract organic (non-paid) traffic. By aligning your content with the algorithms and ranking factors used by search engines like Google, Bing, and Yahoo, you can increase your visibility and attract more visitors to your site.

Key Elements of SEO

- **Keywords**: Identify relevant keywords and phrases that your target audience is searching for. Incorporate these keywords strategically into your content, including titles, headings, meta descriptions, and body text.
- **Content Quality**: Create high-quality, valuable content that addresses the needs and interests of your audience. Aim for comprehensive, well-researched content that provides depth and value.

- **On-Page Optimization**: Optimize various on-page elements, such as title tags, meta descriptions, headings, and URL structures, to make your content more search engine-friendly.
- **Off-Page Factors**: Build backlinks from reputable websites to improve your site's authority and credibility. Focus on earning natural, high-quality backlinks through content promotion, outreach, and relationship building.
- **User Experience**: Provide a seamless and user-friendly experience on your website, including fast loading times, mobile responsiveness, and intuitive navigation. A positive user experience can contribute to higher search rankings.

Content Optimization Strategies

To maximize your content's visibility and discoverability, consider the following optimization strategies:

Keyword Research

- **Identify Relevant Keywords**: Use keyword research tools like Google Keyword Planner, SEMrush, or Ahrefs to identify relevant keywords and phrases related to your content topic.
- **Long-Tail Keywords**: Target long-tail keywords—more specific phrases with lower search volume but higher intent—to capture highly targeted traffic.
- **Competitor Analysis**: Analyze competitor websites to identify keywords they're ranking for and uncover new keyword opportunities.

On-Page Optimization

- **Optimize Titles and Meta Descriptions**: Craft compelling titles and meta descriptions that accurately describe your content and entice users to click.
- **Use Headers and Subheadings**: Structure your content using headers (H1, H2, H3) to improve readability and signal the importance of key topics to search engines.
- **Optimize Image Alt Text**: Use descriptive alt text for images to improve accessibility and provide context for search engines.

Content Creation Best Practices

- **Create Comprehensive Content**: Write in-depth, comprehensive content that thoroughly covers the topic and provides value to readers. Aim for content that is unique, informative, and engaging.
- **Use Multimedia Elements**: Incorporate multimedia elements such as images, videos, infographics, and interactive features to enhance the user experience and make your content more engaging.
- **Update and Refresh Content**: Regularly update and refresh your content to keep it relevant and up-to-date. This can improve its visibility in search results and attract returning visitors.

Link Building and Promotion

- **Build High-Quality Backlinks**: Earn backlinks from authoritative websites in your industry or niche to improve your site's authority and credibility. Focus on creating valuable content that naturally attracts links from other sites.

- **Content Promotion**: Promote your content through social media, email marketing, influencer outreach, and content syndication to increase its visibility and attract more traffic.
- **Participate in Online Communities**: Engage with online communities, forums, and Q&A sites related to your niche to establish your expertise, build relationships, and attract traffic to your site.

Technical SEO

- **Optimize Site Speed**: Improve your website's loading speed by optimizing images, minifying CSS and JavaScript files, and leveraging browser caching. A fast-loading website enhances user experience and can lead to higher search rankings.
- **Mobile Optimization**: Ensure your website is optimized for mobile devices to provide a seamless browsing experience for mobile users. Google's mobile-first indexing prioritizes mobile-friendly websites in search results.
- **Fix Technical Issues**: Regularly audit your website for technical issues such as broken links, duplicate content, and crawl errors. Addressing these issues can improve your site's crawlability and indexing by search engines.

Measuring Success with SEO Metrics

To evaluate the effectiveness of your SEO efforts, monitor key metrics and performance indicators:

- **Organic Traffic**: Track the amount of organic traffic your website receives from search engines over time. Monitor changes in traffic volume and patterns.
- **Keyword Rankings**: Monitor your rankings for target keywords and phrases in search engine results pages. Track changes in rankings and identify opportunities for improvement.
- **Backlink Profile**: Analyze your website's backlink profile to identify new backlinks, lost links, and changes in domain authority over time.
- **Conversion Rates**: Measure the impact of organic traffic on conversions, such as sign-ups, purchases, or inquiries. Monitor conversion rates and identify areas for optimization.

Optimizing your content for search and discovery is a continuous process that requires ongoing attention and effort. By implementing effective SEO strategies and techniques, you can improve your content's visibility, attract more organic traffic, and ultimately achieve your business goals. Stay informed about the latest trends and best practices in SEO, and continually refine your approach to adapt to changes in search engine algorithms and user behavior. With dedication and persistence, you can position your content for success in the competitive online landscape.

4.1 Keyword Research for YouTube

Keyword research is a fundamental aspect of optimizing your YouTube content for search and discovery. By identifying relevant keywords and phrases that your target audience is searching for, you can increase the visibility of your videos and attract more viewers. In this section, we'll explore the process of conducting keyword research specifically for YouTube.

Understanding YouTube's Search Algorithm

YouTube's search algorithm determines which videos appear in search results and related video recommendations. While YouTube's algorithm considers various factors, including video relevance, engagement, and viewer behavior, keywords play a crucial role in determining a video's visibility.

Steps for Keyword Research

- **Brainstorm Seed Keywords**: Start by brainstorming a list of seed keywords related to your video topic. These are general terms or phrases that describe the main theme or subject of your video.
- **Use YouTube Autosuggest**: Enter your seed keywords into the YouTube search bar and observe the autosuggest feature. YouTube autosuggest provides keyword suggestions based on popular search queries, giving you insights into what people are searching for.
- **Explore Related Keywords**: After entering a seed keyword, scroll down to the bottom of the search results page to find related keywords and phrases. These suggestions can help you discover additional relevant keywords to target.
- **Utilize Keyword Research Tools**: Take advantage of keyword research tools like YouTube's own Keyword Planner, as well as third-party tools like TubeBuddy, VidIQ, and Keywords Everywhere. These tools provide data on search volume,

competition, and related keywords, helping you identify high-potential keywords to target.

- **Analyze Competitor Keywords**: Analyze the keywords used in the titles, descriptions, and tags of videos from competitors or creators in your niche. Identify common keywords and topics that are driving traffic to their videos.
- **Consider Long-Tail Keywords**: Long-tail keywords are longer, more specific phrases that have lower search volume but higher intent. Targeting long-tail keywords can help you attract highly relevant traffic and compete against larger channels.

Keyword Optimization Tips

- **Prioritize Relevance**: Choose keywords that are highly relevant to your video content. Optimize your titles, descriptions, and tags with keywords that accurately describe the topic and content of your video.
- **Include Keywords Naturally**: Incorporate your target keywords naturally into your video titles, descriptions, and tags. Avoid keyword stuffing, as this can negatively impact the viewer experience and may result in penalties from YouTube.
- **Optimize Video Titles**: Craft compelling and descriptive video titles that include your target keywords. Your title should accurately reflect the content of your video and entice viewers to click.
- **Write Detailed Descriptions**: Write detailed and informative video descriptions that provide context and additional information about your video. Include relevant keywords naturally throughout the description to improve search visibility.

- **Tag Strategically**: Use relevant keywords as tags to help YouTube understand the content and context of your video. Include both broad and specific tags to cover various aspects of your video content.

Monitor and Iterate

Keyword research is an ongoing process, and it's essential to monitor the performance of your videos and adjust your keyword strategy accordingly. Pay attention to metrics like search impressions, and click-through rate (CTR), and watch time to gauge the effectiveness of your keyword optimization efforts. Continuously iterate on your keyword strategy based on performance data and evolving trends in your niche.

By conducting thorough keyword research and optimizing your YouTube content with relevant keywords, you can improve the visibility and discoverability of your videos, attract more viewers, and grow your YouTube channel. Keep experimenting with different keywords and strategies to find what works best for your content and audience.

4.2 Crafting SEO-Friendly Titles and Descriptions

Crafting SEO-friendly titles and descriptions is crucial for optimizing your content to rank higher in search engine results pages (SERPs) and attract more viewers. In this section, we'll explore strategies for creating titles and descriptions that are both engaging for viewers and optimized for search engines.

Title Optimization

Your video title is the first thing viewers see when browsing search results, so it's essential to make it captivating and informative. Here's how to optimize your titles for SEO:

- **Include Target Keywords**: Incorporate relevant keywords naturally into your title to improve its visibility in search results. Place the most important keywords towards the beginning of the title for maximum impact.
- **Be Descriptive**: Clearly describe the content of your video in the title to help viewers understand what they can expect. Use descriptive language that entices viewers to click while accurately representing the video's content.
- **Keep it Concise**: Aim for a concise and to-the-point title that communicates the main topic or theme of your video succinctly. Avoid unnecessary filler words or phrases that don't add value.
- **Add Emotional Appeal**: Consider incorporating emotional triggers or power words into your title to evoke curiosity, excitement, or urgency. Emotionally resonant titles are more likely to capture viewers' attention and compel them to watch.
- **Test Different Variations**: Experiment with different variations of your title to see which performs best in terms of click-through rate (CTR) and search visibility. Use A/B testing to compare different titles and refine your approach over time.

Description Optimization

Your video description provides additional context and information about your video, helping both viewers and search engines understand its content. Here's how to optimize your descriptions for SEO:

- **Include Keywords Naturally**: Incorporate relevant keywords naturally throughout your description to improve its visibility in search results. Write in a conversational tone and avoid keyword stuffing, as this can detract from the user experience.
- **Provide Value**: Use the description to provide valuable information about your video, such as a summary of the content, key points, or additional resources. Include timestamps for different sections of the video to make it more navigable.
- **Optimize Length**: Aim for a description that is neither too short nor too long. A description of around 200-300 words is generally sufficient to provide adequate context without overwhelming viewers.
- **Include Links**: Add relevant links to other videos, playlists, or external resources in your description to encourage further engagement and exploration. Use descriptive anchor text for hyperlinks to provide clarity and context.
- **Call to Action (CTA)**: Include a clear call to action at the end of your description to prompt viewers to take action, such as subscribing to your channel, liking the video, or visiting your website.
- **Use Formatting**: Break up your description into paragraphs and use formatting options like bullet points or numbered lists to improve readability. This makes it easier for viewers to scan the description and find the information they're looking for.

Monitor Performance and Iterate

After optimizing your titles and descriptions, monitor their performance using analytics tools to see how they impact your video's visibility and engagement. Pay attention to metrics like search impressions, and CTR, and watch time to gauge the effectiveness of your optimization efforts. Continuously iterate on your titles and descriptions based on performance data and viewer feedback to refine your SEO strategy over time.

By crafting SEO-friendly titles and descriptions that are both informative and engaging, you can improve the visibility and discoverability of your videos, attract more viewers, and ultimately grow your audience on YouTube. Keep experimenting with different approaches and optimizing your content to stay ahead in the competitive digital landscape.

4.3 Effective Use of Tags and Hashtags

Tags and hashtags are powerful tools for improving the discoverability and searchability of your content on platforms like YouTube and social media. In this section, we'll explore how to effectively use tags and hashtags to optimize your content for search and discovery.

Tags on YouTube

Tags are keywords or phrases that help YouTube's algorithm understand the content of your video and categorize it appropriately. Here's how to use tags effectively on YouTube:

- **Relevant Keywords**: Choose tags that are directly relevant to the content of your video. Include both broad and specific tags to cover various aspects of your video's topic.
- **Target Keywords**: Prioritize target keywords that have high search volume and relevance to your audience. Use tools like YouTube's autocomplete feature and keyword research tools to identify popular keywords and phrases.
- **Long-Tail Keywords**: Incorporate long-tail keywords—more specific phrases with lower search volume but higher intent—into your tags to capture highly targeted traffic.
- **Variety of Tags**: Include a variety of tags that encompass different aspects of your video's content, including main topics, subtopics, related terms, and variations. This helps your video appear in a wider range of search queries.
- **Monitor Performance**: Monitor the performance of your tags using YouTube Analytics to see which tags are driving traffic to your videos. Adjust your tag strategy based on performance data and trends in your niche.

Hashtags on Social Media

Hashtags are clickable keywords or phrases preceded by the "#" symbol, used to categorize and discover content on social media platforms like Twitter, Instagram, and LinkedIn. Here's how to effectively use hashtags on social media:

- **Relevant and Specific**: Choose hashtags that are relevant to the content of your post and specific to your audience and niche.

Avoid using overly generic hashtags that are too broad and competitive.

- **Research Popular Hashtags**: Research popular hashtags related to your topic or industry using tools like Hashtagify, RiteTag, or social media analytics platforms. Look for hashtags with a balance of popularity and relevance.
- **Create Branded Hashtags**: Consider creating branded hashtags unique to your brand or campaign. Branded hashtags can help increase brand awareness, encourage user-generated content, and foster community engagement.
- **Use Trending Hashtags**: Monitor trending hashtags and timely topics relevant to your audience and participate in relevant conversations. Incorporate trending hashtags into your posts to increase visibility and reach.
- **Limit the Number of Hashtags**: Use hashtags sparingly and strategically, focusing on quality over quantity. Research suggests that posts with fewer hashtags tend to perform better in terms of engagement.
- **Mix Popular and Niche Hashtags**: Include a mix of popular, widely-used hashtags and niche, industry-specific hashtags in your posts. This helps your content reach a broader audience while also targeting a more specific, engaged audience.

Best Practices for Tags and Hashtags

- **Consistency**: Use consistent tags and hashtags across your content to establish a cohesive brand identity and make it easier for users to find related content.
- **Experimentation**: Experiment with different tags and hashtags to see what resonates best with your audience and drives the most

engagement. Monitor performance metrics to identify patterns and trends.

- **Stay Relevant**: Regularly review and update your tags and hashtags to ensure they remain relevant to your content and audience. Trends and topics can change quickly, so stay informed and adapt your strategy accordingly.
- **Engage with Communities**: Engage with communities and conversations related to your niche using relevant hashtags. Participate in discussions, share valuable content, and connect with like-minded individuals to expand your reach and network.

By effectively using tags and hashtags, you can improve the discoverability and searchability of your content on platforms like YouTube and social media, attract more viewers and engagement, and grow your audience and brand presence online. Experiment with different strategies, monitor performance metrics and refine your approach over time to maximize the impact of your tags and hashtags.

4.4 Optimizing Thumbnails for Click-Through Rates

Thumbnails are the first visual impression viewers have of your video, making them crucial for attracting clicks and driving engagement. In this section, we'll explore strategies for optimizing thumbnails to improve click-through rates (CTRs) and maximize the visibility of your content.

Importance of Thumbnails

Thumbnails serve as a preview of your video, providing viewers with a glimpse of its content and enticing them to click and watch. An eye-catching thumbnail can significantly impact CTRs, leading to more views, longer watch times, and improved performance in search and recommendation algorithms.

Tips for Thumbnail Optimization

Here are some tips for optimizing your thumbnails to maximize click-through rates:

- **Use High-Quality Images**: Use clear, high-resolution images for your thumbnails to ensure they look professional and visually appealing. Avoid blurry or pixelated images that may deter viewers from clicking.
- **Feature Faces and Expressions**: Incorporate faces and expressive facial expressions in your thumbnails to evoke emotion and capture viewers' attention. Research shows that thumbnails with human faces tend to perform better in terms of engagement.
- **Highlight Key Visuals**: Choose visuals that accurately represent the content and main focus of your video. Highlight key visuals, scenes, or elements that are compelling and relevant to the topic.
- **Add Text Overlay**: Include concise text overlay on your thumbnails to provide context, convey your video's value proposition, or highlight key points. Use bold, easy-to-read fonts and contrasting colors to make the text stand out.
- **Maintain Branding Consistency**: Maintain consistency in branding elements such as colors, fonts, logos, and visual style across your thumbnails. This helps viewers recognize your content and builds brand recognition over time.
- **Optimize Thumbnail Composition**: Pay attention to composition and layout when designing your thumbnails. Use the rule of thirds,

leading lines, and focal points to create visually balanced and engaging thumbnails.

- **Test Different Variations**: Experiment with different thumbnail designs, images, and text overlays to see which variations perform best in terms of CTRs and engagement. Use A/B testing or split testing to compare different thumbnail designs and iterate based on performance data.

Thumbnail Best Practices

- **Keep it Simple**: Avoid cluttering your thumbnails with too many elements or text. Keep the design clean, uncluttered, and easy to digest at a glance.
- **Optimize for Mobile**: Ensure your thumbnails are optimized for mobile viewing, where a significant portion of YouTube traffic comes from. Use clear, legible text and avoid overly intricate designs that may be difficult to discern on smaller screens.
- **Maintain Relevance**: Ensure your thumbnails accurately represent the content of your video and provide a clear indication of what viewers can expect. Misleading thumbnails can lead to disappointed viewers and lower engagement rates.
- **Monitor Performance**: Track the performance of your thumbnails using YouTube Analytics to see which designs and variations are driving the highest CTRs and engagement rates. Use this data to inform future thumbnail optimization efforts.

4.5 Utilizing YouTube Analytics to Improve Discoverability

YouTube Analytics provides valuable insights into the performance of your videos, audience demographics, and traffic sources, helping you make informed decisions to improve discoverability and engagement. In this section, we'll explore how to leverage YouTube Analytics effectively to optimize your content strategy and grow your audience.

Key Metrics to Monitor

YouTube Analytics offers a wide range of metrics and data points to track the performance of your videos. Here are some key metrics to monitor:

- **Watch Time**: Watch time measures the total amount of time viewers spend watching your videos. It's a crucial metric that influences YouTube's algorithm and search rankings.
- **Audience Retention**: Audience retention shows how well your video retains viewers' attention over time. Aim for high audience retention rates to keep viewers engaged and watching your videos for longer durations.
- **Traffic Sources**: Traffic sources indicate where your viewers are coming from, such as YouTube searches, suggested videos, external websites, or direct traffic. Understanding your traffic sources can help you identify opportunities to optimize your video promotion and distribution strategy.
- **Demographics**: Audience demographics provide insights into the age, gender, location, and interests of your viewers. Use this

information to tailor your content and messaging to better resonate with your target audience.

- **Engagement Metrics**: Engagement metrics like likes, comments, shares, and subscriber growth indicate how viewers are interacting with your content. Monitor engagement metrics to gauge audience feedback and sentiment.

Analyzing Performance Trends

In addition to tracking individual video metrics, it's essential to analyze performance trends and patterns over time. Look for trends in watch time, audience retention, and engagement metrics to identify which types of content resonate best with your audience.

- **Content Performance**: Identify which types of content, topics, or formats perform best in terms of watch time, audience retention, and engagement. Double down on content that consistently performs well and consider producing similar content in the future.
- **Audience Behavior**: Analyze audience behavior trends, such as viewing habits, preferences, and demographics. Use this information to tailor your content strategy and distribution channels to better meet the needs and interests of your audience.
- **Seasonality and Trends**: Pay attention to seasonality and trends in your audience's behavior and interests. Adjust your content calendar and promotion strategy to capitalize on seasonal trends and timely topics that resonate with your audience.

Optimization Opportunities

YouTube Analytics can also help you identify optimization opportunities to improve the discoverability and performance of your videos.

- **Keyword Optimization**: Analyze which keywords and search terms are driving traffic to your videos through YouTube searches. Optimize your metadata, including titles, descriptions, and tags, to better align with popular search queries and improve search visibility.
- **Thumbnail Performance**: Evaluate the performance of your thumbnails by tracking CTRs and audience engagement. Experiment with different thumbnail designs, images, and text overlays to see which variations drive the highest CTRs and viewer engagement.
- **Content Strategy Refinement**: Use audience retention data to identify areas for improvement in your content. Analyze drop-off points and viewer behavior patterns to refine your content strategy and create more engaging videos that keep viewers watching.

Continuous Improvement

YouTube Analytics is a powerful tool for continuously monitoring and optimizing your content strategy to improve discoverability, engagement, and audience growth. Regularly review and analyze your analytics data to identify trends, insights, and areas for improvement. Experiment with different strategies, tactics, and content formats, and iterate based on performance data to continually refine your approach and drive success on YouTube.

Chapter 5: Growing and Engaging Your Audience

Building and engaging a loyal audience is essential for the long-term success of your content strategy. In this chapter, we'll explore strategies and techniques for growing your audience and fostering meaningful engagement with your viewers.

Understanding Audience Growth

Audience growth involves attracting new viewers to your content while retaining and nurturing existing followers. Here are some key strategies for growing your audience:

1. Consistent Content Creation

Consistency is key to building an audience. Regularly publish high-quality content that resonates with your target audience's interests and preferences. Establish a content schedule and stick to it to maintain audience engagement and loyalty.

2. Cross-Promotion and Collaboration

Collaborate with other creators in your niche or industry to reach new audiences and expand your reach. Cross-promote each other's content through collaborations, shoutouts, or guest appearances to tap into each other's audience bases.

3. Audience Engagement and Interaction

Engage with your audience regularly by responding to comments, questions, and feedback. Foster a sense of community by creating opportunities for audience participation, such as polls, Q&A sessions, or live streams. Show appreciation for your viewers' support and contributions to encourage loyalty and engagement.

4. Promote Your Content

Promote your content across multiple channels and platforms to increase visibility and attract new viewers. Share your videos on social media, forums, and online communities relevant to your niche. Utilize email marketing, newsletters, and website/blog integration to drive traffic to your YouTube channel or content platform.

Maximizing Audience Engagement

Engagement is the key to building a loyal and dedicated audience. Here are some strategies for maximizing audience engagement:

1. Create Interactive Content

Produce interactive content that encourages viewers to participate and engage with your content. Use interactive elements such as polls, quizzes, challenges, or interactive annotations to involve your audience and make them feel invested in your content.

2. Encourage User-generated Content (UGC)

Encourage your audience to create and share their content related to your brand or content theme. Feature user-generated content in your videos, social media posts, or community highlights to foster a sense of belonging and recognition among your audience.

3. Host Live Events and Q&A Sessions

Host live events, Q&A sessions, or live streams to connect with your audience in real time. Use live chat and audience interaction features to engage with viewers, answer questions, and address their comments and concerns directly.

4. Personalize Your Content

Tailor your content to your audience's interests, preferences, and feedback. Use viewer analytics and feedback to understand your audience's demographics, viewing habits, and content preferences, and create content that resonates with their needs and desires.

Measuring Audience Growth and Engagement

Track and measure key metrics to gauge the effectiveness of your audience growth and engagement efforts. Monitor metrics such as subscriber growth, view counts, watch time, likes, comments, shares, and audience retention to assess the impact of your content strategy and engagement initiatives.

Growing and engaging your audience requires a combination of consistency, creativity, and genuine interaction. By consistently producing high-quality content, collaborating with other creators, fostering audience engagement, and monitoring key metrics, you can build a loyal and dedicated audience that supports and advocates for your brand or content platform. Stay attentive to your audience's needs and preferences, and continually adapt and refine your content strategy to nurture meaningful relationships and foster a thriving community around your content.

5.1 Building a Community: Responding to Comments and Feedback

Building a thriving community around your content is crucial for fostering engagement, loyalty, and long-term success. One of the most effective ways to nurture this community is by actively engaging with your audience through comments and feedback. In this section, we'll explore strategies for effectively responding to comments and feedback to build a strong and engaged community.

Importance of Engaging with Comments

Responding to comments and feedback demonstrates that you value and appreciate your audience's input. It fosters a sense of connection and belonging, encouraging viewers to become more invested in your content and brand. Additionally, engaging with comments can spark conversations, encourage repeat visits, and improve overall engagement metrics.

Strategies for Responding to Comments

Here are some strategies for effectively engaging with comments and feedback:

- **Be Prompt**: Respond to comments promptly to show that you're actively involved and interested in engaging with your audience. Aim to respond to comments as soon as possible, ideally within the first 24-48 hours of posting.
- **Be Genuine and Authentic**: Respond to comments genuinely and authentically. Show appreciation for positive feedback, address questions or concerns sincerely, and acknowledge constructive criticism with humility and openness.
- **Personalize Responses**: Personalize your responses to make viewers feel valued and appreciated. Address commenters by name if possible, and tailor your responses to their specific questions, feedback, or contributions.
- **Encourage Conversation**: Encourage conversation and interaction by asking questions, soliciting opinions, or inviting viewers to share their experiences or insights related to the content. Create a welcoming and inclusive environment where viewers feel comfortable engaging with each other as well as with you.
- **Handle Negative Feedback Professionally**: Handle negative feedback or criticism professionally and constructively. Avoid responding defensively or engaging in arguments with detractors. Instead, address concerns empathetically, acknowledge valid points, and seek to resolve issues amicably.

- **Set Boundaries**: While engaging with comments is important, it's also essential to set boundaries and manage your time effectively. Prioritize responding to comments that contribute to meaningful conversations or require a response, and consider using filters or moderation tools to manage spam or inappropriate comments.

Leveraging Feedback to Inform Content

In addition to responding to comments, leverage feedback from your audience to inform your content strategy and improve the quality of your content. Pay attention to recurring themes, suggestions, or requests in comments and feedback, and use this insight to create content that resonates with your audience's interests and preferences.

Responding to comments and feedback is a powerful way to build a sense of community, foster engagement, and strengthen relationships with your audience. By actively engaging with comments, demonstrating authenticity and appreciation, and leveraging feedback to inform your content strategy, you can cultivate a loyal and engaged community that supports and advocates for your brand or content platform. Keep the conversation going, listen to your audience, and continue to nurture meaningful connections to create a thriving community around your content.

5.2 Collaborations and Influencer Partnerships

Collaborating with other creators and forming influencer partnerships can be a powerful strategy for expanding your reach, attracting new audiences, and fostering engagement within your community. In this section, we'll explore the benefits of collaborations and influencer partnerships, as well as strategies for forming successful partnerships.

Benefits of Collaborations and Influencer Partnerships

- **Expanded Reach**: Collaborating with other creators or influencers allows you to tap into their existing audience and reach new viewers who may be interested in your content or brand.
- **Credibility and Trust**: Partnering with reputable influencers or established creators can lend credibility and trust to your brand or content, as their endorsement can influence their followers' perceptions and attitudes towards your content.
- **Diversified Content**: Collaborations enable you to create diverse and innovative content by leveraging the unique perspectives, skills, and expertise of other creators. This can help keep your content fresh and engaging for your audience.
- **Cross-Promotion Opportunities**: Collaborations often involve cross-promotion, where both parties promote each other's content to their respective audiences. This can lead to increased visibility, engagement, and subscriber growth for both collaborators.

Strategies for Successful Collaborations

- **Identify Compatible Partners**: Choose collaborators whose content aligns with your brand values, target audience, and content niche. Look for creators or influencers whose audience demographics and interests complement yours.
- **Build Genuine Relationships**: Approach potential collaborators with a genuine interest in their content and a willingness to build a

mutually beneficial relationship. Take the time to engage with their content, interact with them on social media, and establish rapport before proposing collaboration ideas.

- **Define Clear Objectives**: Clearly define your objectives and expectations for the collaboration, including the goals you hope to achieve, the type of content you want to create, and the target audience you want to reach. Ensure that both parties are aligned and committed to the collaboration's success.

- **Collaborate on Content Creation**: Collaborate closely with your partner on content creation, brainstorming ideas, planning the execution, and ensuring that the final product aligns with both parties' brands and objectives. Be open to compromise and flexibility to accommodate each other's creative vision and preferences.

- **Promote and Amplify**: Once the collaboration is live, promote and amplify the content across both collaborators' channels and platforms. Utilize social media, email newsletters, and other marketing channels to maximize visibility and engagement.

- **Measure and Evaluate**: Track the performance of the collaboration using relevant metrics such as views, engagement, subscriber growth, and reach. Evaluate the impact of the collaboration on your key objectives and use this feedback to inform future collaborations and partnerships.

Examples of Collaborative Content

- **Guest Appearances**: Invite a guest creator to appear on your channel or participate in a joint video collaboration.
- **Collaborative Projects**: Partner with other creators to produce collaborative projects such as series, challenges, or tutorials.

- **Product Collaborations**: Collaborate with brands or companies to create sponsored or co-branded content that aligns with both parties' interests and audiences.

Collaborations and influencer partnerships offer valuable opportunities for expanding your reach, attracting new audiences, and fostering engagement within your community. By identifying compatible partners, building genuine relationships, defining clear objectives, collaborating on content creation, and promoting the collaboration effectively, you can create compelling and impactful content that resonates with your audience and drives success for both parties involved. Keep an open mind, be proactive in seeking collaboration opportunities, and leverage the power of partnerships to take your content and community to new heights.

5.3 Utilizing Live Streaming to Connect with Viewers

Live streaming offers a unique and interactive way to connect with your audience in real time, fostering engagement, building relationships, and creating memorable experiences. In this section, we'll explore the benefits of live streaming and strategies for effectively utilizing this powerful tool to connect with viewers.

Benefits of Live Streaming

- **Real-Time Interaction**: Live streaming allows you to engage with your audience in real time, answering questions, responding to comments, and fostering meaningful conversations.

- **Authenticity and Transparency**: Live streaming offers an authentic and unfiltered way to connect with your audience, showcasing your personality, expertise, and behind-the-scenes moments in real time.
- **Increased Engagement**: Live streams tend to attract higher levels of engagement compared to pre-recorded content, as viewers feel a sense of immediacy and connection when interacting with live content.
- **Community Building**: Live streaming fosters a sense of community among your audience, bringing viewers together to participate in shared experiences, discussions, and activities.

Strategies for Successful Live Streaming

- **Plan Ahead**: Plan your live streams, considering factors such as the topic, format, timing, and duration of the stream. Create a compelling title and promotional materials to generate excitement and anticipation among your audience.
- **Interact with Viewers**: Engage with your audience throughout the livestream by responding to comments, answering questions, and acknowledging viewer contributions. Encourage viewer participation through polls, Q&A sessions, and interactive elements.
- **Provide Value**: Offer valuable and engaging content that resonates with your audience's interests and preferences. Whether you're sharing educational content, hosting interviews, or showcasing behind-the-scenes moments, prioritize providing value to your viewers.
- **Be Authentic**: Be yourself and maintain authenticity during the live stream. Show your personality, enthusiasm, and genuine

interest in connecting with your audience. Authenticity builds trust and rapport with your viewers, fostering stronger connections.

- **Promote Your Live Streams**: Promote your live streams across your social media channels, email newsletters, and other marketing platforms to maximize visibility and attract viewers. Use teaser trailers, countdowns, and reminders to build anticipation and excitement leading up to the stream.
- **Optimize Technical Setup**: Ensure your technical setup is optimized for live streaming, including a stable internet connection, high-quality audio and video equipment, and adequate lighting. Test your setup before going live to troubleshoot any potential issues and ensure a smooth streaming experience.

Types of Live Stream Content

- **Q&A Sessions**: Host live Q&A sessions where viewers can ask questions and interact with you in real time.
- **Tutorials and Demonstrations**: Conduct live tutorials, demonstrations, or workshops on topics relevant to your audience's interests.
- **Behind-the-scenes**: Offer a glimpse behind the scenes of your content creation process, sharing insights, challenges, and experiences with your audience.
- **Interviews and Collaborations**: Invite guests or collaborators to join you for live interviews, discussions, or joint content creation sessions.

Live streaming is a powerful tool for connecting with your audience, fostering engagement, and building a loyal community around your content. By planning, interacting with viewers, providing value, maintaining authenticity, promoting your live streams, and optimizing your technical setup, you can create compelling and impactful live content that resonates with your audience and drives success for your brand or content platform. Embrace the opportunities that live streaming offers to connect with your audience in real time, create memorable experiences, and build lasting relationships with your viewers.

5.4 Creating and Managing YouTube Playlists

YouTube playlists are powerful tools for organizing and presenting your content cohesively and engagingly, enhancing discoverability, increasing watch time, and maximizing viewer retention. In this section, we'll explore strategies for creating and managing YouTube playlists effectively to engage your audience and optimize your content strategy.

Benefits of YouTube Playlists

- **Enhanced Organization**: Playlists allow you to organize your videos into thematic collections or series, making it easier for viewers to find and watch related content in one place.
- **Increased Watch Time**: Curating playlists encourages viewers to watch multiple videos in succession, leading to longer watch times and improved engagement metrics.
- **Improved Discoverability**: Optimized playlists can appear in YouTube search results and recommendations, increasing the visibility and reach of your content to new audiences.

- **Content Repurposing**: Playlists enable you to repurpose and repackage your existing content into themed collections, extending the lifespan and value of your videos.

Strategies for Creating Effective Playlists

- **Define Clear Themes**: Create playlists around specific themes, topics, or series to provide viewers with curated collections of related content. Consider your audience's interests and preferences when defining playlist themes.
- **Curate High-Quality Content**: Select high-quality videos that align with the theme of each playlist, prioritizing content that offers value, relevance, and engagement for your audience.
- **Optimize Playlist Titles and Descriptions**: Use descriptive and keyword-rich titles and descriptions for your playlists to improve their visibility in YouTube search results and recommendations. Include relevant keywords and phrases that reflect the content of the playlist.
- **Customize Playlist Thumbnails**: Customize the thumbnails for your playlists to make them visually appealing and distinctive. Use compelling imagery, branding elements, and text overlays to grab viewers' attention and encourage clicks.
- **Arrange Videos Strategically**: Arrange videos within playlists strategically to optimize viewer engagement and retention. Consider factors such as video length, format, and pacing when determining the order of videos within a playlist.

Managing and Promoting Playlists

- **Regularly Update Playlists**: Keep your playlists up-to-date by adding new videos and removing outdated or irrelevant content. Regularly review and refresh your playlists to ensure they remain relevant and engaging for your audience.
- **Cross-Promote Playlists**: Promote your playlists across your YouTube channel, social media platforms, and other marketing channels to increase their visibility and encourage viewers to explore your curated collections of content.
- **Monitor Performance Metrics**: Use YouTube Analytics to track the performance of your playlists, including metrics such as watch time, views, and engagement. Analyze which playlists are driving the most engagement and adjust your playlist strategy accordingly.
- **Experiment with Playlist Formats**: Experiment with different playlist formats, such as curated playlists, series playlists, or collaborative playlists, to see which formats resonate best with your audience and drive the highest engagement.

Examples of Playlist Themes

- **Tutorial Series**: Curate a playlist featuring step-by-step tutorials or instructional videos on a specific topic or skill.
- **Product Reviews**: Create a playlist showcasing reviews and demonstrations of products or services related to your niche or industry.
- **Best of/Top Picks**: Compile a playlist highlighting your best-performing or most popular videos, organized by category or theme.

- **Behind-the-scenes**: Share a behind-the-scenes look at your content creation process, including bloopers, outtakes, and behind-the-scenes footage.

YouTube playlists are valuable tools for organizing, presenting, and promoting your content cohesively and engagingly. By defining clear themes, curating high-quality content, optimizing titles and descriptions, customizing thumbnails, and strategically managing and promoting your playlists, you can enhance discoverability, increase watch time, and maximize viewer engagement on your YouTube channel. Experiment with different playlist formats, themes, and promotion strategies to find what works best for your audience and content goals. Embrace the power of playlists to showcase your content in a compelling and organized way, and leverage their potential to attract and retain viewers on your channel.

5.5 Encouraging User-Generated Content and Challenges

User-generated content (UGC) and challenges are powerful ways to engage your audience, foster community participation, and create a sense of belonging among your viewers. In this section, we'll explore strategies for encouraging UGC and challenges on your content platform.

Benefits of User-Generated Content and Challenges

- **Increased Engagement**: Encouraging viewers to create and share their content fosters active participation and engagement within your community.

- **Authenticity and Relatability**: UGC adds authenticity and relatability to your content, as it showcases real people interacting with and responding to your brand or content.
- **Community Building**: UGC helps build a sense of community among your audience, as viewers connect through shared experiences and interactions.
- **Content Variety**: Incorporating UGC and challenges into your content strategy adds variety and freshness, keeping your audience interested and engaged over time.

Strategies for Encouraging UGC and Challenges

- **Set Clear Guidelines**: Provide clear guidelines and instructions for creating and submitting UGC or participating in challenges. Clearly outline the theme, rules, and submission process to make it easy for viewers to participate.
- **Offer Incentives**: Offer incentives or rewards for participating in UGC or challenges, such as shoutouts, prizes, or featured placement in your content. Incentives can motivate viewers to participate and increase engagement levels.
- **Promote Participation**: Actively promote UGC and challenges across your content platform, social media channels, and other marketing channels to encourage participation. Use teasers, announcements, and reminders to generate excitement and anticipation.
- **Provide Inspiration**: Provide inspiration and examples to spark creativity and encourage participation. Share examples of UGC or challenge submissions from other viewers to showcase the possibilities and inspire others to join in.

- **Facilitate Collaboration**: Encourage collaboration and interaction among participants by creating opportunities for them to connect, share ideas, and collaborate on projects. Foster a supportive and inclusive environment where everyone feels welcome to participate.

Examples of UGC and Challenges

- **Photo or Video Contests**: Invite viewers to submit photos or videos related to a specific theme or topic, such as a favorite travel destination or creative DIY project.
- **Creative Challenges**: Challenge viewers to create and share their interpretations of a creative prompt or theme, such as a drawing challenge or storytelling challenge.
- **Product or Brand Challenges**: Encourage viewers to showcase how they use your products or incorporate your brand into their daily lives through photos, videos, or testimonials.
- **Community Engagement Challenges**: Create challenges that promote community engagement and interaction, such as sharing acts of kindness, participating in charitable initiatives, or spreading positivity online.

By setting clear guidelines, offering incentives, promoting participation, providing inspiration, and facilitating collaboration, you can empower your audience to become active contributors to your content platform. Embrace the creativity and enthusiasm of your viewers, and leverage the power of UGC and challenges to enhance engagement, build community, and create memorable experiences for your audience.

Chapter 6: Promoting Your Videos

Promoting your videos is essential for increasing visibility, attracting new viewers, and maximizing the impact of your content. In this chapter, we'll explore strategies and techniques for effectively promoting your videos to reach a wider audience and drive engagement.

Understanding the Importance of Video Promotion

Promoting your videos is crucial for ensuring that your content gets seen by the right audience and achieves its intended goals. Effective video promotion can help you:

- **Increase Visibility**: Promoting your videos across various channels and platforms increases their visibility and exposure to potential viewers.
- **Attract New Viewers**: By reaching new audiences through targeted promotion, you can attract new viewers who may be interested in your content.
- **Drive Engagement**: Promoted videos are more likely to be watched, liked, shared, and commented on, leading to increased engagement and interaction with your audience.
- **Maximize Impact**: Strategic promotion ensures that your videos reach their full potential and achieve the desired outcomes, whether it's generating leads, driving sales, or raising awareness.

Strategies for Promoting Your Videos

1. Optimize Video Metadata:

Optimize your video titles, descriptions, and tags with relevant keywords to improve search visibility and ranking on YouTube and other search engines.

2. Share on Social Media:

Share your videos across your social media profiles, including Facebook, Twitter, Instagram, and LinkedIn, to reach your existing followers and attract new viewers.

3. Collaborate with Influencers:

Partner with influencers or other content creators in your niche to reach their audience and tap into their existing fanbase.

4. Email Marketing:

Promote your videos to your email subscribers through newsletters, email campaigns, or dedicated video updates to drive traffic to your YouTube channel or website.

5. Utilize Paid Advertising:

Invest in paid advertising on platforms like YouTube Ads, Google Ads, or social media platforms to target specific demographics, interests, and behaviors and reach a wider audience.

6. Engage with Online Communities:

Participate in online communities, forums, and discussion groups relevant to your niche or industry, and share your videos when relevant to attract interested viewers.

7. Optimize for SEO:

Optimize your video titles, descriptions, and tags with relevant keywords and phrases to improve search visibility and ranking on YouTube and search engines.

8. Cross-Promote with Other Content:

Cross-promote your videos within your content, such as links to related videos in end screens or cards, to encourage viewers to explore more of your content.

Measuring Success and Iterating

After implementing your video promotion strategies, it's important to monitor and measure the effectiveness of your efforts. Track metrics such as views, watch time, engagement, and conversions to evaluate the impact of your promotion activities and identify areas for improvement. Use this data to iterate and refine your promotion strategies over time, focusing on tactics that yield the best results and optimizing your approach to maximize the reach and impact of your videos.

Promoting your videos is essential for reaching a wider audience, driving engagement, and maximizing the impact of your content. By implementing strategic promotion strategies such as optimizing video metadata, sharing on social media, collaborating with influencers, utilizing paid advertising, engaging with online communities, optimizing for SEO, and cross-promoting with other content, you can increase visibility, attract new viewers, and achieve your content goals. Continuously monitor and measure the success of your promotion efforts, and iterate based on data and feedback to optimize your video promotion strategy for maximum impact and success.

6.1 Social Media Integration: Sharing Across Platforms

Integrating social media into your video promotion strategy is essential for reaching a broader audience, driving engagement, and maximizing the impact of your content. In this section, we'll explore strategies for effectively sharing your videos across various social media platforms to expand your reach and attract new viewers.

Importance of Social Media Integration

- **Reach New Audiences**: Social media platforms have billions of active users worldwide, providing ample opportunities to reach new audiences and attract viewers who may not be familiar with your content.
- **Drive Traffic**: Sharing your videos on social media channels drives traffic back to your YouTube channel or content platform, increasing views, watch time and engagement metrics.
- **Encourage Engagement**: Social media platforms facilitate two-way communication and interaction with your audience, allowing viewers to like, comment, share, and engage with your content in real time.
- **Build Community**: Social media integration helps foster a sense of community among your audience, as viewers connect and with your brand through shared experiences and interactions.

Strategies for Sharing Across Platforms

- **Tailor Content for Each Platform**: Customize your video promotions for each social media platform to optimize content format, length, and messaging for the specific audience and platform dynamics.
- **Create Teaser Trailers**: Create short teaser trailers or highlights of your videos to share on social media, generating excitement and anticipation among your followers.
- **Share Behind-the-Scenes Content**: Offer a glimpse behind the scenes of your video creation process, sharing insights, bloopers,

or outtakes to provide additional value and engagement on social media.

- **Utilize Stories and Live Features**: Leverage social media features such as Stories and live streaming to promote your videos in real-time, engaging with your audience and driving immediate viewership.
- **Engage with Your Audience**: Actively engage with your audience on social media by responding to comments, questions, and feedback related to your videos, fostering meaningful interactions and relationships.
- **Cross-Promote with Influencers**: Collaborate with influencers or other content creators on social media to cross-promote each other's videos, tapping into their audience and expanding your reach.

Examples of Social Media Integration

- **Facebook**: Share video trailers, behind-the-scenes footage, or live Q&A sessions with your Facebook followers to drive traffic to your YouTube channel or website.
- **Twitter**: Tweet short video clips, GIFs, or quotes from your videos, accompanied by relevant hashtags and mentions to increase visibility and engagement.
- **Instagram**: Post visually appealing images or carousel posts featuring highlights from your videos, accompanied by compelling captions and calls to action to watch the full video.
- **LinkedIn**: Share educational or informative videos related to your industry or niche, targeting professionals and businesses within your network.

Integrating social media into your video promotion strategy is essential for reaching a wider audience, driving engagement, and maximizing the impact of your content. By tailoring content for each platform, creating teaser trailers, sharing behind-the-scenes content, utilizing Stories and live features, engaging with your audience, and cross-promoting with influencers, you can effectively promote your videos across social media platforms and attract new viewers to your content. Embrace the opportunities that social media integration offers to expand your reach, foster engagement, and build a thriving community around your content.

6.2 Email Marketing and Newsletters

Email marketing and newsletters are powerful tools for promoting your videos, driving traffic to your content platform, and nurturing relationships with your audience. In this section, we'll explore strategies for leveraging email marketing and newsletters to effectively promote your videos and engage your subscribers.

Importance of Email Marketing

- **Direct Communication**: Email provides a direct and personal way to communicate with your audience, allowing you to deliver targeted messages and promotions directly to their inbox.
- **Drive Traffic**: Email marketing drives traffic to your videos and content platform by encouraging subscribers to click through to watch your latest videos or explore your website.
- **Build Trust and Loyalty**: Consistent email communication helps build trust and loyalty with your audience, as subscribers become familiar with your brand and content over time.

- **Segmentation and Personalization**: Email marketing allows for segmentation and personalization, enabling you to tailor your messages and promotions to specific audience segments based on their interests, behavior, or preferences.

Strategies for Email Marketing and Newsletters

- **Build a Subscribers List**: Build an email subscribers list by encouraging visitors to your website or content platform to sign up for your newsletter through opt-in forms, pop-ups, or incentives such as exclusive content or discounts.
- **Create Compelling Content**: Craft compelling email content that grabs subscribers' attention and entices them to click through to watch your videos. Use engaging subject lines, clear calls-to-action, and visually appealing designs to drive engagement.
- **Feature Video Highlights**: Showcase highlights of your latest videos or curated playlists in your email newsletters, providing subscribers with a preview of your content and encouraging them to watch more.
- **Segment Your Audience**: Segment your email list based on subscriber preferences, interests, or behavior, and tailor your email content and promotions accordingly. Personalized emails are more likely to resonate with recipients and drive engagement.
- **Include Call-to-Action (CTA)**: Include clear and compelling calls-to-action (CTAs) in your emails, directing subscribers to watch your videos, visit your website, or take specific actions such as sharing your content or leaving comments.
- **Schedule Regular Emails**: Establish a consistent email schedule, whether it's weekly, bi-weekly, or monthly, to keep subscribers

engaged and informed about your latest content, updates, and promotions.

Examples of Email Marketing Content

- **New Video Announcements**: Notify subscribers about your latest video releases or content updates, providing links and previews to encourage clicks and views.
- **Curated Playlists**: Share curated playlists of your top videos, series, or themes, giving subscribers easy access to your best content.
- **Exclusive Content**: Offer subscribers exclusive content, sneak peeks, or behind-the-scenes access to reward their loyalty and encourage engagement.
- **Promotional Offers**: Promote special offers, discounts, or giveaways related to your videos or content platform, incentivizing subscribers to take action.

Email marketing and newsletters are valuable tools for promoting your videos, driving traffic to your content platform, and nurturing relationships with your audience. By building a subscribers list, creating compelling content, segmenting your audience, including clear CTAs, scheduling regular emails, and providing valuable content and offers, you can effectively leverage email marketing to engage your subscribers and drive engagement with your videos. Embrace the power of email marketing to build trust and loyalty with your audience, drive traffic to your content, and achieve your video promotion goals.

6.3 Paid Advertising Options on YouTube

Paid advertising on YouTube offers powerful opportunities to promote your videos, reach targeted audiences, and drive engagement with your content. In this section, we'll explore the various paid advertising options available on YouTube and strategies for effectively leveraging them to maximize the impact of your video promotion efforts.

Importance of Paid Advertising

- **Increased Visibility**: Paid advertising increases the visibility of your videos by promoting them to a wider audience of potential viewers who may not have discovered your content organically.
- **Targeted Reach**: YouTube's advertising platform allows for precise targeting based on demographics, interests, behaviors, and other criteria, ensuring that your videos reach the most relevant audience for your content.
- **Drive Engagement**: Paid advertising drives engagement with your videos by encouraging viewers to watch, like, comment, share, and subscribe, ultimately increasing watch time and improving overall engagement metrics.
- **Measurable Results**: YouTube's advertising platform provides detailed analytics and reporting tools, allowing you to track the performance of your campaigns in real time and measure the effectiveness of your advertising efforts.

Paid Advertising Options on YouTube

TrueView Ads:

- TrueView ads are skippable video ads that appear before, during, or after other YouTube videos.
- Advertisers only pay when viewers choose to watch their ad, making it a cost-effective option for reaching engaged viewers.

Non-Skippable In-Stream Ads:

- Non-skippable in-stream ads are video ads that play before, during, or after other YouTube videos and cannot be skipped by viewers.
- Advertisers pay on a CPM (cost per thousand impressions) basis, making it suitable for maximizing reach and visibility.

Bumper Ads:

- Bumper ads are short, non-skippable video ads that play before, during, or after other YouTube videos and are limited to a maximum length of six seconds.
- Advertisers pay on a CPM basis, and bumper ads are ideal for delivering concise messages or brand awareness campaigns.

Display Ads:

- Display ads are static or animated image ads that appear alongside YouTube videos, on YouTube search results on pages, or within Google Display Network sites and apps.

- Advertisers pay on a CPM or CPC (cost per click) basis, and display ads are effective for increasing brand visibility and driving website traffic.

Overlay Ads:

- Overlay ads are semi-transparent overlay ads that appear on the lower portion of a video while it's playing.
- Advertisers pay on a CPM or CPC basis, and overlay ads are suitable for promoting products, services, or calls-to-action within the video player.

Strategies for Effective Paid Advertising

- **Define Clear Objectives**: Determine your advertising objectives, whether it's increasing brand awareness, driving website traffic, generating leads, or promoting specific videos or content.
- **Target Relevant Audiences**: Utilize YouTube's targeting options to reach the most relevant audience for your content, based on demographics, interests, behaviors, and other criteria.
- **Create Compelling Ads**: Create compelling and engaging video ads that capture viewers' attention, convey your message effectively, and encourage them to take action.
- **Optimize Campaign Performance**: Monitor the performance of your advertising campaigns regularly, analyze key metrics such as views, engagement, click-through rates, and conversions, and adjust your targeting, bidding, and creative elements accordingly to optimize performance.

- **Test and Iterate**: Experiment with different ad formats, targeting options, ad creatives, and bidding strategies to identify what works best for your audience and objectives, and iterate based on data and insights to improve campaign effectiveness over time.

Paid advertising on YouTube offers powerful opportunities to promote your videos, reach targeted audiences, and drive engagement with your content. By leveraging TrueView ads, non-skippable in-stream ads, bumper ads, display ads, and overlay ads, and implementing strategies for defining clear objectives, targeting relevant audiences, creating compelling ads, optimizing campaign performance, and testing and iterating on ad creatives and strategies, you can effectively maximize the impact of your video promotion efforts and achieve your advertising goals on YouTube. Embrace the opportunities that paid advertising offers to increase visibility, drive engagement, and achieve success with your video content.

6.4 Embedding Videos on Your Website and Blog

Embedding videos on your website and blog is a powerful way to showcase your content, engage visitors, and drive traffic to your YouTube channel or content platform. In this section, we'll explore the benefits of embedding videos and strategies for effectively integrating video content into your website and blog.

Benefits of Embedding Videos

- **Enhanced Engagement**: Videos are highly engaging and can capture visitors' attention more effectively than text or images alone, resulting in longer dwell times and increased interaction on your website or blog.

- **Visual Appeal**: Videos add visual appeal to your website or blog, making your content more dynamic, memorable, and shareable, which can help differentiate your site and attract more visitors.
- **Improved SEO**: Embedding videos can improve your website's search engine optimization (SEO) by increasing dwell time, reducing bounce rates, and providing valuable multimedia content that search engines favor in their algorithms.
- **Promotion and Branding**: Embedding videos allows you to promote your brand, products, or services directly on your website or blog, providing visitors with valuable information and promoting brand awareness and recognition.

Strategies for Embedding Videos

- **Choose Relevant Content**: Select videos that are relevant to the content and context of your website or blog post, providing value to visitors and enhancing their overall experience.
- **Optimize Placement**: Place embedded videos strategically within your website or blog post to capture visitors' attention and encourage engagement. Consider embedding videos near the top of the page or within the main content area for maximum visibility.
- **Customize Video Player**: Customize the appearance and functionality of the embedded video player to match your website's design and branding, ensuring a seamless and cohesive user experience.
- **Include Call-to-Action (CTA)**: Include clear and compelling calls-to-action (CTAs) alongside embedded videos, prompting

visitors to take specific actions such as subscribing to your channel, visiting your website, or exploring related content.

- **Provide Context**: Provide context or additional information about embedded videos within your website or blog post, explaining the relevance or purpose of the video and guiding visitors on how to engage with it.
- **Optimize for Mobile**: Ensure that embedded videos are optimized for viewing on mobile devices, as a significant portion of website traffic comes from mobile users. Choose responsive video players that adapt to different screen sizes and resolutions for a seamless viewing experience.

Examples of Embedded Video Content

- **Product Demonstrations**: Embed videos showcasing product demonstrations, tutorials, or customer testimonials to educate and inform visitors about your products or services.
- **Interviews or Webinars**: Embed recorded interviews, webinars, or panel discussions relevant to your industry or niche, providing valuable insights and expertise to your audience.
- **Behind-the-Scenes Footage**: Embed behind-the-scenes footage or vlogs showcasing your team, workspace, or creative process, offering a glimpse into your brand's personality and culture.
- **Educational Content**: Embed educational or informative videos addressing common questions, challenges, or topics of interest to your audience, establishing your expertise and authority in your field.

Embedding videos on your website and blog is an effective strategy for engaging visitors, enhancing your content, and promoting your brand or content platform. By choosing relevant content, optimizing placement, customizing the video player, including clear CTAs, providing context, and optimizing for mobile, you can effectively integrate video content into your website or blog and maximize its impact on your audience. Embrace the power of embedded videos to showcase your content, captivate visitors, and drive engagement with your brand or website.

6.5 Engaging with Online Communities and Forums

Engaging with online communities and forums is a valuable strategy for promoting your videos, connecting with your target audience, and building a strong and active community around your content platform. In this section, we'll explore the benefits of engaging with online communities and forums and strategies for effectively leveraging them to promote your videos and grow your audience.

Benefits of Engaging with Online Communities

- **Targeted Reach**: Online communities and forums attract members with specific interests, hobbies, or demographics, allowing you to reach a highly targeted audience that is likely to be interested in your content.
- **Build Credibility**: Active participation in online communities and forums helps build credibility and authority in your niche or industry, as you contribute valuable insights, expertise, and resources to the community.

- **Increase Visibility**: Engaging with online communities and forums increases the visibility of your content by sharing your videos, participating in discussions, and providing helpful recommendations or solutions to community members.
- **Drive Traffic**: By sharing your videos and promoting your content within online communities and forums, you can drive traffic back to your YouTube channel or content platform, increasing views, engagement, and subscriber growth.

Strategies for Engaging with Online Communities

- **Identify Relevant Communities**: Identify online communities and forums relevant to your niche, industry, or target audience, and prioritize active and engaged communities with a sizable membership.
- **Provide Value**: Focus on providing value to the community by sharing helpful information, insights, and resources related to your expertise or content niche. Avoid self-promotion or spammy tactics and instead aim to genuinely contribute to the community.
- **Share Your Videos**: Share your videos within relevant discussions or threads, providing context and value to community members. Focus on sharing videos that directly address topics or questions being discussed within the community.
- **Participate Actively**: Actively participate in discussions, ask questions, answer queries, and engage with other community members to build rapport and establish yourself as a trusted and respected member of the community.
- **Be Authentic and Genuine**: Be authentic and genuine in your interactions with community members, showing genuine interest in

their interests, concerns, and opinions. Building authentic relationships within the community is key to long-term success.

- **Respect Community Guidelines**: Respect the rules and guidelines of each online community or forum, and adhere to their posting guidelines, etiquette, and code of conduct to maintain a positive and constructive environment.

Examples of Online Communities and Forums

- **Reddit**: Participate in relevant subreddits related to your content niche or industry, sharing your videos, engaging in discussions, and answering questions from community members.
- **Quora**: Provide helpful answers to questions related to your expertise or content niche on Quora, and share your videos when relevant to provide additional value to users seeking information.
- **Facebook Groups**: Join and engage with Facebook groups relevant to your niche, sharing your videos, participating in discussions, and connecting with like-minded individuals.
- **Discord Servers**: Join Discord servers or communities dedicated to topics or interests relevant to your content, and engage with members through text, voice, or video channels.

By identifying relevant communities, providing value, sharing your videos, participating actively, being authentic and genuine, and respecting community guidelines, you can effectively leverage online communities to increase visibility, drive traffic, and grow your audience. Embrace the opportunities that online communities offer to connect with like-minded individuals, share your expertise, and promote your content in a meaningful and authentic way.

Chapter 7: Analyzing Performance and ROI

Analyzing the performance of your video content and assessing the return on investment (ROI) of your video marketing efforts are crucial steps in optimizing your strategy, refining your approach, and maximizing the impact of your content platform. In this chapter, we'll delve into the importance of analyzing performance metrics, strategies for measuring ROI, and tools for tracking and evaluating the effectiveness of your video marketing campaigns.

Importance of Analyzing Performance and ROI

- **Data-Driven Decisions**: Analyzing performance metrics provides valuable insights into how your videos are performing, enabling you to make informed decisions about content creation, distribution, and promotion.
- **Identifying Success Factors**: Performance analysis helps identify which types of videos, topics, formats, or channels resonate most with your audience, allowing you to replicate success and optimize future content.
- **Optimizing ROI**: Measuring ROI helps determine the effectiveness of your video marketing efforts in achieving your business goals, such as increasing brand awareness, driving website traffic, generating leads, or boosting sales.
- **Continuous Improvement**: By continuously monitoring and analyzing performance metrics and ROI, you can identify areas for improvement, refine your strategy, and allocate resources more effectively to maximize the impact of your video content.

Strategies for Analyzing Performance

- **Define Key Performance Indicators (KPIs)**: Identify key performance indicators (KPIs) relevant to your goals and objectives, such as views, watch time, engagement rate, conversion rate, or revenue generated.
- **Utilize Analytics Tools**: Use analytics tools provided by platforms like YouTube, Google Analytics, or social media platforms to track and analyze performance metrics, audience demographics, and engagement patterns.
- **Segmentation and Comparison**: Segment your audience and content by various factors such as demographics, geography, device type, or referral source, and compare performance metrics across different segments to identify trends and insights.
- **A/B Testing**: Conduct A/B tests or experiments to test different variables such as video thumbnails, titles, descriptions, or promotion strategies, and analyze the impact on performance metrics to optimize your content and strategy.
- **Benchmarking and Trend Analysis**: Benchmark your performance against industry standards or competitors, and conduct trend analysis to identify emerging patterns, changes in audience behavior, or shifts in market dynamics.

Measuring ROI of Video Marketing

- **Set Clear Objectives**: Define clear objectives for your video marketing campaigns, whether it's increasing brand awareness, driving website traffic, generating leads, or increasing sales, and establish metrics for measuring success.

- **Track Conversions and Revenue**: Use tracking tools such as conversion tracking pixels, UTM parameters, or affiliate tracking codes to attribute conversions and revenue directly to your video marketing efforts and calculate ROI.
- **Calculate Cost Per Acquisition (CPA)**: Calculate the cost per acquisition (CPA) by dividing the total cost of your video marketing campaign by the number of conversions or acquisitions generated, providing a measure of cost-effectiveness.
- **Evaluate Lifetime Value (LTV)**: Consider the lifetime value (LTV) of customers acquired through your video marketing efforts, factoring in repeat purchases, referrals, or long-term engagement to assess the true impact on ROI.

Tools for Tracking and Evaluation

- **YouTube Analytics**: YouTube Analytics provides detailed insights into your channel's performance, including views, watch time, audience demographics, and engagement metrics, helping you understand how viewers interact with your content.
- **Google Analytics**: Google Analytics offers comprehensive website analytics, including traffic sources, user behavior, and conversion tracking, allowing you to track the impact of your video marketing efforts on website traffic and conversions.
- **Social Media Insights**: Social media platforms like Facebook, Twitter, and Instagram provide analytics dashboards with performance metrics such as reach, engagement, and click-through rates, enabling you to track the effectiveness of video promotion on social media.
- **Third-Party Analytics Tools**: Third-party analytics tools such as Hootsuite, Sprout Social, or SEMrush offer advanced analytics and

reporting capabilities, allowing you to track and analyze performance across multiple channels and platforms in one centralized dashboard.

Analyzing the performance of your video content and measuring the ROI of your video marketing efforts are essential steps in optimizing your strategy, refining your approach, and maximizing the impact of your content platform. By defining key performance indicators (KPIs), utilizing analytics tools, conducting segmentation and comparison analysis, and measuring ROI through conversions and revenue tracking, you can gain valuable insights into audience behavior, content effectiveness, and campaign success. Embrace the power of data-driven decision-making to continuously improve your video marketing strategy, drive business results, and achieve your content goals.

7.1 Key Metrics to Track: Views, Watch Time, and Engagement

Tracking key metrics is essential for understanding the performance of your video content and evaluating the effectiveness of your video marketing efforts. In this section, we'll explore three key metrics that are crucial for measuring the success of your videos: views, watch time, and engagement.

Views

- **Definition**: Views represent the number of times your video has been watched by viewers. Each time a viewer initiates playback of your video, it counts as one view.

- **Importance**: Views indicate the reach and exposure of your video content. Higher view counts suggest greater audience interest and visibility.
- **Tracking and Analysis**: Monitor the total number of views for each video, as well as the growth trends over time. Analyze factors such as video titles, thumbnails, and promotion strategies that contribute to increases or decreases in views.

Watch Time

- **Definition**: Watch time refers to the total amount of time that viewers have spent watching your videos. It is measured in minutes or hours.
- **Importance**: Watch time is a critical metric that reflects audience engagement and content quality. Longer watch times indicate that viewers find your content valuable and are more likely to watch it in its entirety.
- **Tracking and Analysis**: Track the watch time for each video and analyze the average watch duration to understand viewer behavior. Identify segments or topics that capture viewers' interest and optimize your content to maintain audience engagement throughout the video.

Engagement

- **Definition**: Engagement metrics include likes, comments, shares, and subscriber actions such as subscriptions, notifications, and playlist additions.

- **Importance**: Engagement metrics reflect the level of interaction and connection between your audience and your content. Higher engagement signals active viewer participation and indicates that your content resonates with your audience.
- **Tracking and Analysis**: Monitor engagement metrics for each video, including likes, comments, shares, and subscriber actions. Analyze the type and sentiment of comments, as well as the frequency of shares and likes, to gauge audience sentiment and identify opportunities for community engagement and interaction.

Tracking key metrics such as views, watch time, and engagement is essential for evaluating the performance of your video content and assessing the effectiveness of your video marketing efforts. By monitoring these metrics closely, you can gain valuable insights into audience behavior, content quality, and campaign success, enabling you to optimize your strategy, refine your approach, and achieve your content goals. Embrace the power of data-driven decision-making to drive continuous improvement and maximize the impact of your video content.

7.2 Understanding YouTube Analytics Reports

YouTube Analytics provides valuable insights into the performance of your channel and individual videos, allowing you to track key metrics, understand audience behavior, and optimize your content strategy. In this section, we'll explore the various reports available in YouTube Analytics and how to interpret them effectively.

Overview Report

- **Description**: The Overview report provides a summary of your channel's performance, including key metrics such as views, watch time, subscribers, and revenue.
- **Insights**: Use the Overview report to track overall channel growth trends, identify spikes or dips in performance, and assess the impact of recent content uploads or promotional activities.

Watch Time Report

- **Description**: The Watch Time report provides detailed insights into how much time viewers have spent watching your videos, broken down by video, date, and geography.
- **Insights**: Use the Watch Time report to identify which videos have the highest watch time and average view duration, understand audience retention patterns, and optimize your content to maximize watch time.

Traffic Sources Report

- **Description**: The Traffic Sources report shows where your viewers are coming from, including YouTube search, suggested videos, external websites, and YouTube features such as the homepage or subscription feed.
- **Insights**: Use the Traffic Sources report to identify which sources are driving the most traffic to your videos, optimize your video

metadata and promotion strategies for key traffic sources, and expand your reach by targeting new traffic sources.

Audience Retention Report

- **Description**: The Audience Retention report visualizes how viewers engage with your videos over time, showing when viewers drop off or stop watching.
- **Insights**: Use the Audience Retention report to identify which parts of your videos are most engaging and which segments experience viewer drop-off. Optimize your content to maintain audience interest and retention throughout the video.

Demographics Report

- **Description**: The Demographics report provides demographic information about your audience, including age, gender, and geographic location.
- **Insights**: Use the Demographics report to understand the composition of your audience, tailor your content and messaging to resonate with specific demographic segments and identify opportunities to reach new audience demographics.

Revenue Report

- **Description**: The Revenue report shows how much money your channel has earned from ad revenue, YouTube Premium revenue, Super Chat, and channel memberships.

- **Insights**: Use the Revenue report to track your channel's monetization performance, identify revenue trends over time, and optimize your monetization strategies to maximize earnings.

YouTube Analytics offers a wealth of data and insights to help you understand and optimize the performance of your channel and videos. By leveraging reports such as the Overview, Watch Time, Traffic Sources, Audience Retention, Demographics, and Revenue reports, you can gain valuable insights into audience behavior, content effectiveness, and revenue generation. Use these insights to inform your content strategy, refine your approach, and achieve your channel goals effectively. Embrace the power of YouTube Analytics to drive continuous improvement and maximize the impact of your video content.

7.3 Conducting A/B Testing for Thumbnails and Titles

A/B testing is a valuable technique for optimizing the performance of your videos by testing different variations of thumbnails and titles to determine which ones resonate most with your audience. In this section, we'll explore the process of conducting A/B testing for thumbnails and titles effectively.

Importance of A/B Testing

- **Data-Driven Decisions**: A/B testing allows you to make data-driven decisions about your video thumbnails and titles, based on real audience feedback and engagement metrics.

- **Optimization**: By testing different variations, you can identify which thumbnails and titles attract more clicks, views, and engagement, ultimately optimizing your content for maximum impact.
- **Continuous Improvement**: A/B testing is an ongoing process that enables you to continuously refine and improve your video thumbnails and titles over time, keeping your content fresh and relevant to your audience.

Steps for Conducting A/B Testing

- **Define Hypotheses**: Start by defining clear hypotheses or assumptions about which elements of your thumbnails and titles you want to test. For example, you might hypothesize that a brighter thumbnail background will attract more attention than a darker background.
- **Create Variations**: Create multiple variations of thumbnails and titles, each with a single variable or element that you want to test. For example, you might create variations of thumbnails with different background colors or text placements.
- **Randomize and Test**: Randomly assign each variation to different versions of your video and monitor their performance over a set period. Ensure that the testing conditions are consistent and that external factors do not skew the results.
- **Measure Performance**: Track key metrics such as click-through rate (CTR), view count, watch time, and engagement rate for each variation. Analyze the data to determine which variations perform best and meet your objectives.
- **Draw Conclusions**: Based on the results of the A/B test, draw conclusions about which thumbnails and titles are most effective in

attracting viewers and driving engagement. Use these insights to inform future content creation and optimization strategies.

Best Practices for A/B Testing

- **Focus on One Variable**: Test one variable at a time to isolate its impact on performance. This allows you to accurately assess the effectiveness of each element and make informed decisions.
- **Test Sufficient Sample Size**: Ensure that your A/B test includes a sufficient sample size to yield statistically significant results. Aim for a large enough sample to minimize the margin of error and draw reliable conclusions.
- **Be Patient**: A/B testing requires patience and consistency. Allow enough time for the test to run and gather meaningful data before drawing conclusions or making changes to your content strategy.
- **Iterate and Iterate**: Use the insights gained from A/B testing to iterate and refine your thumbnails and titles continuously. Experiment with new variations and strategies to keep optimizing your content for maximum impact.

Tools for A/B Testing

- **YouTube Studio**: YouTube Studio provides built-in tools for A/B testing thumbnails and titles, allowing you to upload multiple variations and monitor their performance directly within the platform.
- **Third-Party Tools**: There are also third-party tools and software available specifically for A/B testing video thumbnails and titles,

offering advanced analytics and optimization features for creators and marketers.

A/B testing is a powerful technique for optimizing the performance of your video content by testing different variations of thumbnails and titles. By defining clear hypotheses, creating multiple variations, measuring performance metrics, and drawing conclusions based on data, you can identify which thumbnails and titles resonate most with your audience and drive maximum engagement. Embrace the process of A/B testing as an essential component of your content optimization strategy, and use the insights gained to continuously improve and refine your video thumbnails and titles for optimal results.

7.4 Measuring the ROI of Your YouTube Marketing Efforts

Measuring the return on investment (ROI) of your YouTube marketing efforts is essential for assessing the effectiveness of your strategy and demonstrating the value of your content platform. In this section, we'll explore the process of measuring ROI for your YouTube marketing efforts and the key metrics to consider.

Importance of Measuring ROI

- **Demonstrating Value**: Measuring ROI allows you to quantify the impact of your YouTube marketing efforts in terms of tangible outcomes, such as revenue generated, leads generated, or brand awareness.

- **Optimization**: By understanding the ROI of different marketing activities, you can identify which strategies are most effective and allocate resources more efficiently to maximize returns.
- **Decision Making**: ROI analysis provides valuable insights for making data-driven decisions about future investments in YouTube marketing, content creation, and promotional activities.

Steps for Measuring ROI

Set Clear Objectives: Define clear and specific objectives for your YouTube marketing efforts, such as increasing brand awareness, driving website traffic, generating leads, or boosting sales.

Track Key Metrics: Identify key performance indicators (KPIs) that align with your objectives and track them consistently over time. These metrics may include views, watch time, engagement, conversions, revenue, and customer acquisition cost (CAC).

Attribute Conversions: Use tracking tools such as conversion tracking pixels, UTM parameters, or affiliate tracking codes to attribute conversions directly to your YouTube marketing efforts. This allows you to measure the impact of your videos on driving conversions and revenue.

Calculate ROI: Calculate the ROI of your YouTube marketing efforts by comparing the return (e.g., revenue generated) to the investment (e.g., production costs, advertising spending). The ROI formula is:

$$\text{ROI} = \frac{\text{Return} - \text{Investment}}{\text{Investment}} \times 100\%$$

Analyze the ROI for different campaigns, videos, or promotional activities to understand which strategies deliver the highest returns.

Key Metrics to Consider

- **Views and Watch Time**: Measure the number of views and total watch time generated by your videos to gauge their reach and engagement with your audience.
- **Engagement Metrics**: Track engagement metrics such as likes, comments, shares, and click-through rates (CTR) to assess viewer interaction and interest in your content.
- **Conversions and Revenue**: Monitor conversions, sales, and revenue generated as a result of your YouTube marketing efforts to understand the direct impact on your bottom line.
- **Customer Acquisition Cost (CAC)**: Calculate the cost per acquisition (CAC) by dividing the total investment in YouTube marketing by the number of conversions or customers acquired. Compare CAC to the lifetime value (LTV) of customers to assess profitability.

Tools for Measuring ROI

- **YouTube Analytics**: YouTube Analytics provides insights into video performance, audience demographics, and engagement metrics, allowing you to track key metrics and assess the impact of your content.
- **Google Analytics**: Google Analytics offers advanced tracking and reporting capabilities for measuring website traffic, conversions, and revenue generated from YouTube referrals.

- **CRM and E-commerce Platforms**: Integrate your CRM or e-commerce platform with YouTube Analytics to track conversions, sales, and customer data directly from your website or online store.

Measuring the ROI of your YouTube marketing efforts is essential for evaluating the effectiveness of your strategy, optimizing resource allocation, and demonstrating the value of your content platform. By setting clear objectives, tracking key metrics, attributing conversions, and calculating ROI, you can gain valuable insights into the impact of your YouTube marketing activities and make informed decisions to drive business results. Embrace the process of ROI analysis as a critical component of your content strategy and use the insights gained to continuously improve and optimize your YouTube marketing efforts for maximum impact and returns.

7.5 Making Data-Driven Decisions for Future Content

Data-driven decision-making is essential for optimizing your content strategy on YouTube and ensuring that your content resonates with your audience effectively. In this section, we'll explore how to leverage data to make informed decisions for future content creation.

Importance of Data-Driven Decision-Making

- **Audience Understanding**: Data provides valuable insights into audience preferences, behavior, and engagement patterns, allowing you to understand what content resonates most with your viewers.

- **Optimization**: By analyzing performance metrics and audience feedback, you can identify areas for improvement and optimize your content strategy to better meet the needs and interests of your audience.
- **Content Relevance**: Data-driven decisions help ensure that your content remains relevant and engaging, keeping your audience interested and invested in your channel over time.

Steps for Making Data-Driven Decisions

- **Analyze Performance Metrics**: Start by analyzing performance metrics such as views, watch time, engagement rate, and audience retention for your existing videos. Identify trends, patterns, and outliers that can inform your content strategy.
- **Understand Audience Demographics**: Use demographic data provided by YouTube Analytics to understand the composition of your audience, including age, gender, location, and interests. Tailor your content to resonate with your target demographic segments.
- **Listen to Audience Feedback**: Pay attention to comments, likes, dislikes, and other forms of audience feedback to understand viewer preferences, interests, and pain points. Use this feedback to guide content creation and address audience needs.
- **Experiment and Test**: Experiment with different types of content, formats, topics, and styles to see what resonates best with your audience. Conduct A/B testing for thumbnails, titles, and video formats to optimize engagement and click-through rates.
- **Iterate and Refine**: Continuously monitor performance metrics and audience feedback, and use these insights to iterate and refine your content strategy over time. Stay agile and adapt to changing audience preferences and market trends.

Key Metrics to Consider

- **Views and Watch Time**: Measure the number of views and total watch time generated by your videos to gauge their reach and engagement with your audience.
- **Engagement Metrics**: Track engagement metrics such as likes, comments, shares, and click-through rates (CTR) to assess viewer interaction and interest in your content.
- **Audience Retention**: Analyze audience retention metrics to understand how well your content holds viewers' attention over time and identify areas for improvement.
- **Conversion and Revenue**: Monitor conversions, sales, and revenue generated as a result of your content to assess its impact on driving business outcomes.

Tools for Data Analysis

- **YouTube Analytics**: YouTube Analytics provides detailed insights into video performance, audience demographics, and engagement metrics, allowing you to track key metrics and assess the impact of your content.
- **Google Analytics**: Google Analytics offers advanced tracking and reporting capabilities for measuring website traffic, conversions, and revenue generated from YouTube referrals.
- **Social Listening Tools**: Use social listening tools to monitor conversations and sentiment around your content on social media platforms, helping you understand audience perception and sentiment.

Data-driven decision-making is essential for optimizing your content strategy on YouTube and ensuring that your content resonates with your audience effectively. By analyzing performance metrics, understanding audience demographics, listening to audience feedback, experimenting with different content formats, and iterating based on insights gained, you can continuously improve and refine your content strategy to drive engagement, retention, and growth on your channel. Embrace the power of data to make informed decisions for future content creation and achieve your content goals effectively.

Chapter 8: Advanced Strategies for Boosting Sales

In this chapter, we'll delve into advanced strategies for leveraging your YouTube channel to drive sales and maximize revenue. By implementing these techniques, you can enhance your marketing efforts, increase conversions, and achieve your sales objectives effectively.

Importance of Boosting Sales on YouTube

- **Revenue Generation**: Boosting sales on YouTube allows you to monetize your content and generate revenue directly from your audience through product sales, affiliate marketing, or sponsored content.
- **Audience Engagement**: By offering products or services related to your content niche, you can deepen engagement with your audience and provide additional value beyond your video content.
- **Business Growth**: Increased sales can lead to business growth and expansion opportunities, allowing you to scale your operations, invest in new initiatives, and achieve long-term success.

Advanced Sales Strategies

- **Strategic Product Placement**: Integrate product mentions, endorsements, or demonstrations seamlessly into your video content to promote products or services authentically and effectively.
- **Affiliate Marketing Programs**: Partner with affiliate marketing programs to promote third-party products or services relevant to

your audience. Earn commissions for each sale or referral generated through your affiliate links.

- **Branded Merchandise**: Create and sell branded merchandise such as apparel, accessories, or digital products related to your content or brand. Use platforms like Teespring, Spreadshop, or Shopify to set up online stores and sell merchandise directly to your audience.

- **Sponsored Content and Partnerships**: Collaborate with brands or companies for sponsored content opportunities, where you promote their products or services in exchange for compensation or other benefits. Ensure that sponsored content aligns with your audience's interests and adds value to your channel.

- **Exclusive Offers and Discounts**: Offer exclusive discounts, promotions, or special offers to your YouTube audience as a reward for their loyalty and engagement. Use unique discount codes or affiliate links to track sales generated from your YouTube channel.

- **Launch Product Reviews or Demos**: Create in-depth product reviews, demonstrations, or tutorials to showcase the features, benefits, and uses of products or services. Provide valuable insights and recommendations to help viewers make informed purchasing decisions.

Metrics to Track

- **Conversion Rate**: Monitor the conversion rate for sales-related actions, such as clicks on affiliate links, purchases, or sign-ups. Analyze conversion data to optimize your sales funnel and improve conversion rates over time.

- **Revenue Generated**: Track the total revenue generated from product sales, affiliate commissions, sponsored content, or other monetization strategies. Set revenue goals and measure progress towards achieving them.

- **Audience Engagement**: Measure audience engagement metrics such as watch time, likes, comments, and shares for sales-related content. Assess audience feedback and sentiment to gauge the effectiveness of your sales strategies.
- **Return on Investment (ROI)**: Calculate the ROI for your sales initiatives by comparing the revenue generated to the investment (e.g., time, resources, advertising spend) required to implement them. Optimize strategies with the highest ROI to maximize profitability.

Implementing advanced strategies for boosting sales on YouTube requires a strategic approach, creativity, and a deep understanding of your audience's preferences and needs. By integrating product placements, affiliate marketing, branded merchandise, sponsored content, exclusive offers, and product reviews into your content strategy, you can effectively monetize your channel and drive revenue growth. Continuously track key metrics, analyze performance data, and optimize your sales strategies to maximize conversions, revenue, and overall success on YouTube. Embrace the opportunities for sales and monetization on YouTube, and leverage your channel as a powerful platform for driving business growth and achieving your sales objectives.

8.1 Creating Product Demos and Tutorials

Product demos and tutorials are powerful tools for showcasing the features, benefits, and uses of products or services to your audience on

YouTube. In this section, we'll explore how to create engaging and effective product demos and tutorials to drive sales and boost revenue.

Importance of Product Demos and Tutorials

- **Educate Your Audience**: Product demos and tutorials provide valuable information and insights to your audience, helping them understand how to use a product effectively and make informed purchasing decisions.
- **Build Trust**: By demonstrating products in action and providing honest reviews or recommendations, you can build trust and credibility with your audience, increasing their confidence in the products you promote.
- **Drive Sales**: Well-executed product demos and tutorials can lead to increased interest, engagement, and ultimately, sales conversions as viewers are inspired to purchase the showcased products.

Best Practices for Creating Product Demos and Tutorials

- **Know Your Audience**: Understand the preferences, interests, and needs of your audience to create relevant and valuable product demos and tutorials that resonate with them.
- **Research and Preparation**: Conduct thorough research on the product or service you're showcasing, familiarizing yourself with its features, benefits, and use cases. Plan your demo or tutorial content to ensure clarity and effectiveness.
- **Focus on Benefits**: Highlight the key benefits and value propositions of the product, emphasizing how it can solve

problems or address pain points for your audience. Show real-world examples and scenarios to illustrate the product's practical applications.

- **Keep it Engaging**: Make your demos and tutorials engaging and visually appealing by using high-quality visuals, demonstrations, animations, and on-screen graphics. Keep the pace lively and maintain viewer interest throughout the video.
- **Provide Actionable Insights**: Offer practical tips, tricks, and insights to help viewers get the most out of the product. Share your personal experiences, recommendations, and best practices to enhance the educational value of the content.
- **Be Transparent**: Maintain transparency and authenticity in your demos and tutorials by providing honest reviews, disclosing any sponsorships or affiliations, and addressing potential limitations or drawbacks of the product.
- **Include Calls to Action (CTAs)**: Encourage viewers to take action by including clear and compelling calls to action (CTAs) throughout the video, such as visiting a website, making a purchase, or signing up for a free trial.

Examples of Product Demos and Tutorials

- **Unboxing Videos**: Showcasing the unboxing and initial impressions of a product, highlighting its packaging, contents, and first impressions.
- **How-to Guides**: Providing step-by-step instructions on how to use a product or perform specific tasks related to it, such as assembly, setup, or troubleshooting.

- **Comparison Reviews**: Comparing the features, performance, and value of different products within the same category to help viewers make informed purchasing decisions.
- **Use Case Demonstrations**: Demonstrating real-world use cases and scenarios where the product can be applied effectively, showcasing its versatility and practicality.

Creating compelling product demos and tutorials is an effective strategy for educating your audience, building trust, and driving sales on YouTube. By following best practices, focusing on audience needs, and providing valuable insights and recommendations, you can create engaging and informative content that inspires viewers to take action and make purchases. Embrace the opportunity to showcase products authentically and creatively, and leverage the power of product demos and tutorials to enhance your content strategy and achieve your sales objectives effectively.

8.2 Integrating CTAs and Interactive Elements

Integrating clear calls to action (CTAs) and interactive elements into your YouTube videos is crucial for driving viewer engagement, guiding audience behavior, and ultimately, boosting sales. In this section, we'll explore how to effectively incorporate CTAs and interactive elements into your videos to encourage viewer interaction and drive conversions.

Importance of CTAs and Interactive Elements

- **Guiding Viewer Behavior**: CTAs and interactive elements provide clear instructions and prompts to viewers, guiding them towards desired actions such as subscribing, liking, commenting, or making a purchase.
- **Enhancing Engagement**: Interactive elements such as polls, quizzes, annotations, and end screens make videos more engaging and interactive, encouraging viewers to actively participate and interact with the content.
- **Driving Conversions**: Well-executed CTAs can lead to increased conversions and sales by directing viewers to take specific actions such as visiting a website, signing up for a newsletter, or making a purchase.

Best Practices for Integrating CTAs

- **Be Clear and Direct**: Use clear and concise language to communicate your CTAs, ensuring that viewers understand what action you want them to take. Avoid ambiguity and make it easy for viewers to follow through on your prompts.
- **Placement and Timing**: Strategically place CTAs at key moments throughout your video where viewers are most likely to be receptive, such as at the beginning, middle, or end. Consider the flow of your content and align CTAs with relevant topics or transitions.
- **Visual Design**: Make your CTAs visually appealing and attention-grabbing by using contrasting colors, bold typography, and compelling graphics. Ensure that CTAs stand out from the rest of the content and are easily noticeable.
- **Provide Incentives**: Offer incentives or rewards to incentivize viewers to take action, such as exclusive discounts, freebies, or

access to bonus content. Create a sense of urgency or FOMO (fear of missing out) to motivate immediate action.

- **Customize for Different Platforms**: Tailor CTAs to the specific platform or device where your videos will be viewed, optimizing them for mobile devices, desktops, or smart TVs. Consider platform-specific features such as end screens, cards, or annotations on YouTube.

Examples of Interactive Elements

- **End Screens and Cards**: Use YouTube's end screens and cards feature to add interactive elements such as clickable links, subscribe buttons, or recommended videos at the end of your video.
- **Polls and Surveys**: Incorporate polls or surveys into your videos to gather feedback from viewers, solicit opinions, or gauge audience preferences on specific topics or products.
- **Clickable Annotations**: Create clickable annotations within your videos to direct viewers to related content, external websites, or specific actions such as subscribing or making a purchase.
- **Interactive Overlays**: Use interactive overlays or pop-ups to highlight key information, display product details, or offer additional resources such as downloadable guides or checklists.

Integrating clear calls to action (CTAs) and interactive elements into your YouTube videos is essential for driving viewer engagement, guiding audience behavior, and boosting sales. By following best practices, providing incentives, and customizing CTAs for different platforms, you can effectively encourage viewer interaction and drive conversions. Experiment with different types of CTAs and interactive elements to see what resonates best with your audience, and continuously optimize your approach to maximize engagement and sales on YouTube. Embrace the power of CTAs and interactive elements as powerful tools for enhancing your content strategy and achieving your sales objectives effectively.

8.3 Leveraging YouTube Shopping and Merch Shelf

YouTube Shopping and Merch Shelf are powerful features that allow creators to showcase products directly within their videos and channel, providing seamless opportunities for viewers to discover, explore, and purchase merchandise or products. In this section, we'll explore how to leverage YouTube Shopping and Merch Shelf effectively to drive sales and monetize your content.

Importance of YouTube Shopping and Merch Shelf

- **Monetization Opportunities**: YouTube Shopping and Merch Shelf provide creators with additional revenue streams through product sales, affiliate marketing, and branded merchandise.
- **Enhanced Viewer Experience**: By integrating shopping experiences directly into videos and channel pages, creators can enhance the viewer experience and make it easier for viewers to discover and purchase products featured in their content.
- **Audience Engagement**: Interactive shopping experiences encourage viewer engagement and interaction, as viewers can explore products, read reviews, and make purchases without leaving the YouTube platform.

How to Leverage YouTube Shopping and Merch Shelf

- **Set Up Your Merch Shelf**: Enable the Merch Shelf feature on your YouTube channel to showcase your branded merchandise, products, or affiliated items directly beneath your videos. Customize your shelf with high-quality images, descriptions, and pricing information to entice viewers.

- **Curate Featured Products**: Select featured products to showcase on your Merch Shelf, highlighting new releases, bestsellers, or products relevant to your audience's interests. Rotate featured items regularly to keep your shelf fresh and engaging.

- **Integrate Shopping Cards**: Use YouTube's shopping cards feature to add clickable product links and annotations to your videos, allowing viewers to explore and purchase products featured in your content directly from the video player.

- **Optimize Product Descriptions**: Write compelling and informative product descriptions that highlight key features, benefits, and use cases. Use persuasive language and calls to action to encourage viewers to click through and make a purchase.

- **Promote Exclusive Offers**: Offer exclusive discounts, promotions, or bundles to incentivize viewers to purchase your Merch Shelf. Create a sense of urgency or scarcity to motivate immediate action.

- **Cross-Promote on Social Media**: Promote your Merch Shelf and featured products across your social media channels to reach a wider audience and drive traffic to your YouTube channel and videos.

Best Practices for Success

- **Align with Your Brand**: Ensure that the products featured on your Merch Shelf align with your brand identity and resonate with your audience's interests and preferences.
- **Provide Value**: Offer products that provide value to your audience and complement your content. Focus on quality, relevance, and authenticity to build trust and credibility with your viewers.
- **Monitor Performance**: Regularly monitor the performance of your Merch Shelf and featured products using YouTube Analytics. Track metrics such as clicks, conversions, and revenue to assess the effectiveness of your merchandising efforts.
- **Iterate and Experiment**: Experiment with different product offerings, pricing strategies, and promotional tactics to optimize your merchandising strategy over time. Iterate based on audience feedback and performance data to maximize sales and revenue.

YouTube Shopping and Merch Shelf offer creators powerful tools for monetizing their content and driving sales directly from their videos and channel pages. By leveraging these features effectively, creators can enhance the viewer experience, generate additional revenue streams, and build stronger connections with their audience. Embrace the opportunities provided by YouTube Shopping and Merch Shelf to showcase your products, engage your audience, and achieve your sales objectives effectively on the platform.

8.4 Utilizing YouTube for Lead Generation

YouTube is not only a platform for sharing videos but also a powerful tool for generating leads for your business. By creating compelling content and strategically capturing viewer interest, you can attract potential customers and guide them through your sales funnel. In this section, we'll explore how to effectively utilize YouTube for lead generation.

Importance of Lead Generation on YouTube

- **Building a Customer Base**: Generating leads on YouTube helps you build a database of potential customers who have shown interest in your products or services.
- **Nurturing Relationships**: Lead generation allows you to nurture relationships with your audience through personalized communication, ultimately driving conversions and sales.
- **Measurable ROI**: Effective lead generation strategies can provide measurable returns on investment by tracking how many leads convert into paying customers.

Strategies for Effective Lead Generation

- **Create Valuable Content**: Develop high-quality, informative, and engaging content that addresses the needs and interests of your target audience. Focus on topics that provide solutions, educate, or entertain, ensuring that viewers find value in your videos.

- **Use Clear CTAs**: Include clear and compelling calls to action (CTAs) in your videos to prompt viewers to take specific actions, such as visiting your website, signing up for a newsletter, downloading a free resource, or filling out a contact form.
- **Offer Lead Magnets**: Provide lead magnets, such as free ebooks, checklists, templates, or exclusive access to webinars, in exchange for viewers' contact information. Highlight the benefits of these resources to entice viewers to take action.
- **Optimize Video Descriptions**: Use the video description section to include links to landing pages, contact forms, or lead capture forms. Write persuasive descriptions that encourage viewers to click through and provide their information.
- **Utilize YouTube Cards and End Screens**: Leverage YouTube's interactive features, such as cards and end screens, to promote lead magnets and direct viewers to lead capture pages. These tools can be used to insert clickable links and CTAs within your videos.
- **Create a Compelling Channel Trailer**: Design an engaging channel trailer that introduces new visitors to your channel, highlights your value proposition, and includes a strong CTA for lead generation.
- **Engage with Your Audience**: Actively engage with viewers by responding to comments, answering questions, and participating in discussions. Building rapport and trust with your audience can encourage them to provide their contact information.
- **Promote Your Videos**: Promote your videos across social media platforms, email newsletters, and your website to drive more traffic to your YouTube channel. The more viewers you attract, the higher the potential for lead generation.

Tracking and Measuring Lead Generation Success

- **Use Analytics Tools**: Utilize YouTube Analytics and other tracking tools to monitor the performance of your lead generation efforts. Track key metrics such as video views, click-through rates, and conversion rates to assess the effectiveness of your strategies.
- **Implement UTM Parameters**: Use UTM parameters in your video links to track the source of traffic and leads. This helps you identify which videos and CTAs are driving the most conversions.
- **Integrate with CRM Systems**: Integrate YouTube with your customer relationship management (CRM) system to capture and manage leads efficiently. Automate follow-up processes and track lead progress through your sales funnel.
- **A/B Testing**: Conduct A/B testing with different video content, CTAs, and lead magnets to determine what resonates best with your audience. Use the insights gained to optimize your lead generation strategy continuously.

Utilizing YouTube for lead generation requires a strategic approach, focused content creation, and effective use of CTAs and lead magnets. By providing valuable content, engaging with your audience, and leveraging YouTube's interactive features, you can attract and capture leads, nurture relationships, and drive conversions. Continuously track and measure your lead generation efforts to refine your strategy and maximize your results. Embrace the potential of YouTube as a powerful tool for building your customer base and achieving your business objectives.

8.5 Case Studies: Success Stories and Lessons Learned

Case studies provide valuable insights into successful strategies and highlight practical lessons learned from real-world experiences. In this section, we'll explore a few notable case studies that demonstrate the effective use of YouTube for boosting sales and generating leads. These success stories will offer inspiration and actionable takeaways to help you enhance your own YouTube strategy.

Case Study 1: Blendtec - "Will It Blend?"

Background:

Blendtec, a company known for its high-performance blenders, launched a YouTube series titled "Will It Blend?" The series features the company's founder, Tom Dickson, blending various unconventional items to demonstrate the power and durability of Blendtec blenders.

Strategy:

- **Engaging Content**: The videos are entertaining, featuring a unique concept that blends humor and shock value.
- **Consistent Branding**: Each video highlights the Blendtec brand, emphasizing the product's capabilities memorably.
- **Clear CTAs**: The videos include CTAs directing viewers to the company's website to learn more about the blenders and make a purchase.

Results:

- **Increased Brand Awareness**: The series went viral, significantly increasing brand visibility.
- **Boosted Sales**: Blendtec saw a dramatic increase in sales, attributed to the engaging and shareable nature of the content.
- **Subscriber Growth**: The channel gained millions of subscribers, providing a large audience for future marketing efforts.

Lessons Learned:

- **Creativity Pays Off**: Innovative and entertaining content can capture attention and drive engagement.
- **Consistency is Key**: Regularly posting content that aligns with your brand can build a loyal audience.
- **Effective CTAs Drive Sales**: Clear and compelling CTAs can convert viewers into customers.

Case Study 2: Dollar Shave Club - Viral Launch Video

Background:

Dollar Shave Club (DSC) is a subscription-based service offering affordable razor blades delivered to customers' doors. DSC launched with a humorous YouTube video titled "Our Blades Are F***ing Great."

Strategy:

- **Humor and Personality**: The video uses humor and a casual tone to connect with viewers and differentiate DSC from traditional razor brands.
- **Clear Value Proposition**: It clearly explains the benefits of the service, emphasizing convenience and cost savings.
- **Strong CTA**: The video directs viewers to sign up for the subscription service on the DSC website.

Results:

- **Viral Success**: The launch video quickly went viral, generating millions of views.
- **Rapid Growth**: DSC experienced rapid subscriber growth and significant media attention.
- **Acquisition**: The brand's success led to its acquisition by Unilever for $1 billion.

Lessons Learned:

- **Bold Marketing Works**: Taking risks with bold, humorous content can lead to viral success.
- **Clear Messaging**: Communicating the value proposition helps viewers understand the benefits of your product or service.
- **Strong Launch Strategy**: A well-executed launch video can drive massive initial growth and long-term success.

Case Study 3: Pat Flynn - Smart Passive Income

Background:

Pat Flynn, an entrepreneur and online business expert, uses his YouTube channel "Smart Passive Income" to share tips, tutorials, and case studies about building online businesses and generating passive income.

Strategy:

- **Educational Content**: Flynn provides valuable, actionable advice and insights through tutorials, interviews, and case studies.
- **Lead Magnets**: He offers free resources, such as ebooks and webinars, in exchange for viewers' contact information.
- **Engaging with Audience**: Flynn actively engages with his audience by responding to comments and hosting live Q&A sessions.

Results:

- **Increased Leads**: Flynn's YouTube channel has been a significant source of leads for his email list and online courses.
- **Established Authority**: He has built a reputation as an authority in the online business niche, leading to speaking engagements and partnerships.
- **Steady Revenue**: Flynn generates steady revenue through course sales, affiliate marketing, and sponsored content.

Lessons Learned:

- **Value-Driven Content**: Providing high-quality, valuable content builds trust and authority.
- **Effective Use of Lead Magnets**: Offering free resources can effectively capture leads and grow your email list.
- **Audience Engagement**: Actively engaging with your audience fosters community and loyalty.

These case studies highlight the diverse strategies and creative approaches that can lead to success on YouTube. Whether through engaging and entertaining content, bold and humorous marketing, or valuable and educational videos, these examples demonstrate the potential of YouTube to boost sales and generate leads. By learning from these success stories and applying their lessons to your strategy, you can enhance your YouTube presence, engage your audience, and achieve your business objectives effectively.

Conclusion:

In this comprehensive guide, we've journeyed through the multifaceted world of YouTube marketing, exploring the strategies and techniques that can elevate your brand, grow your audience, increase engagement, and boost sales. As we conclude, let's recap the essential takeaways and the transformative potential that YouTube holds for your marketing efforts.

The Power of YouTube Marketing

YouTube is a dynamic and versatile platform that offers unparalleled opportunities for businesses and creators. It is not just a place to share videos but a powerful tool to connect with a global audience, build a community, and drive business growth. From content creation and optimization to audience engagement and performance analysis, mastering YouTube marketing can significantly impact your brand's success.

Key Strategies and Insights

- **Content Creation Mastery:**

Identifying your target audience is the foundation of effective content creation. Understanding their needs, preferences, and behaviors helps tailor content that resonates and engages.

Planning and scripting engaging videos ensure your content is compelling and retains viewer attention. High production quality, including lighting, sound, and camera work, enhances viewer experience.

Editing your videos like a pro with the right software and techniques can transform raw footage into polished content that stands out.

- **Optimization for Search and Discovery:**

Conducting thorough keyword research and crafting SEO-friendly titles and descriptions are crucial for increasing your content's visibility.

Effective use of tags, hashtags, and optimized thumbnails can boost your click-through rates and overall discoverability.

Leveraging YouTube analytics helps refine your strategy, ensuring your content reaches and resonates with the right audience.

- **Audience Growth and Engagement:**

Building a community through active engagement, responding to comments, and encouraging feedback fosters loyalty and trust.

Collaborations and influencer partnerships can expand your reach and introduce your content to new audiences.

Utilizing live streaming, managing playlists, and encouraging user-generated content and challenges keep your audience engaged and invested in your brand.

- **Promotional Strategies:**

Integrating social media and email marketing amplifies your reach and drives traffic to your YouTube channel.

Exploring paid advertising options on YouTube can target specific demographics, enhancing your promotional efforts.

Embedding videos on your website and engaging with online communities and forums can further boost visibility and engagement.

- **Performance Analysis and ROI:**

Tracking key metrics such as views, watch time, and engagement provides insights into your content's performance.

Understanding YouTube analytics reports and conducting A/B testing for thumbnails and titles helps optimize your strategy.

Measuring the ROI of your marketing efforts ensures you are making data-driven decisions to enhance future content and campaigns.

The Path Forward

The landscape of YouTube marketing is continually evolving, presenting new challenges and opportunities. By staying informed about trends, experimenting with new formats, and continuously engaging with your audience, you can adapt and thrive in this dynamic environment. Remember, the key to success lies in the consistent delivery of value, authenticity, and engagement.

Final Thoughts

YouTube marketing is a powerful avenue for brands and creators to connect with audiences, share their stories, and drive meaningful results. By applying the strategies outlined in this guide, you can harness the full potential of YouTube to elevate your brand, grow your audience, increase engagement, and boost sales. Embrace the creativity, analytics, and community-building aspects of YouTube marketing, and you will find yourself on the path to sustained success.

Thank you for embarking on this journey with us. Now, it's time to put these strategies into action and watch your YouTube channel and brand flourish. Happy creating!

www.ingramcontent.com/pod-product-compliance
Lightning Source LLC
Chambersburg PA
CBHW082233220526

45479CB00005B/1218